RIVERS *of* COURAGE *and* DOUBT

D0067436

NICHOLAS ISIKA

TRUE DIRECTIONS

AN AFFILIATE OF TARCHER BOOKS

RIVERS OF COURAGE AND DOUBT

iUniverse books may be ordered through booksellers or by contacting:

iUniverse
1663 Liberty Drive
Bloomington, IN 47403
www.iuniverse.com
1-800-Authors (1-800-288-4677)

ISBN: 978-1-4917-3358-5 (sc)
ISBN: 978-1-4917-3359-2 (e)

Library of Congress Control Number: 2014908110

Printed in the United States of America.

iUniverse rev. date: 6/11/2014

Contents

Appendix: Copies of correspondence and documents for coming to the United States

Introduction

When I decided to come to school at the Augustana Academy in Canton, South Dakota, I didn't know how I was going to fulfill that dream. I had a plan and a purpose to attend school in the United States, and I made up my mind to pursue it. I kept my dream alive by taking action each day until I finally succeeded. February 6, 1967, I found myself, a teenager, in New York City, newly arrived from Kenya, East Africa, with forty-five dollars in my pocket and at the start of a new life in America.

As I went through my struggle to come to the academy from my home in Kenya, I faced many ups and downs. The downs were more frequent than the ups. I learned from my gracious parents, who did not know how to read or write but who had much wisdom, that "the mind that won't quit through hard times and refuses to sit and wait, but applies action instead, is the mind that will succeed."

Throughout my struggle to come to school in the United States, I faced a lot of discouragement from others. Many times I could not sleep well because I felt I had everything against me on this journey.

I have always been a reader, and one day I found this quotation:

> Road to Success
> The road to success is not straight,
> There is curve failure,
> A loop called confusion,
> Speed bumps called friends,
> Red lights called enemies,
> Caution lights called family.
> You will have flats called jobs.
> But, if you have a spare called determination,
> An engine called perseverance,
> Insurance called faith,
> A driver called God,
> You will make it to a place called success.
> Here is a quote and do not know the author.

The struggle to come to the United States began when I was a young teenager. I could not tell my parents I had this plan because I was the one supporting our whole family in Kenya. Being the oldest son, I was bound by our culture to help my parents, my grandparents, and all my siblings. I was the one responsible for keeping food on the table and meeting all their needs. I loved my parents at all costs. My grandpa Tumbo used to say, "He may say he loves you. Wait and see what he does for you!" And so it was difficult having a dream that threatened to leave behind these duties to my loved ones.

After I left, my two brothers-in-law took on my family responsibility for food and other things. My brother-in-law Samson, especially, had a big heart in helping my parents. Mind you, at the Augustana Academy, I had two jobs. I worked cleaning the main hall during the day, and I also worked in a factory from three in the afternoon to midnight. Then I went home to the dormitory to study until two in the morning. I sent as much money as I could home to my mom to feed the family throughout my time in high school and college in South Dakota.

Every corner I turned on the way to the United States had blockages, but my question always was, "What is the next larger thing?" In other words, "What is my alternative?" I did not want to go backward but to keep moving forward to a better life. I did not want to live with decayed dreams like 95 percent of the world population. I felt I had to do much better than living with regret. I did not want to give up because failure in my life's dream would be a big regret.

The person who expects nothing will never be disappointed. I always expected to succeed in attaining my dream someday. If we let ourselves get discouraged, we will stop fighting for success. When we set a goal to accomplish and we get going to accomplish it, then we face challenges. When we stop pursuing solutions to those challenges, we have to quit our dream.

When you have a goal to shoot for, never stop taking action because of the challenges that arise. Keep on doing more and more to achieve your goal instead. If you doubt yourself, listen to Alexandre Dumas: "A person who doubts himself is like a man who enlists in the ranks of his enemy and bears arms against himself." Don't let regrets replace your dreams.

Tim Redmond cautions, "Don't commit treason against your own life and purpose." When you have a dream, or dreams and goals, your own mind will be your biggest foe. You will face obstacles along the way, but don't let them stop you from pursuing your dream.

Yes, I had an incessant dream to come to school at Augustana Academy. I wound up coming to high school, instead of college, because when I left Kenya I had only an eighth-grade education. At Augustana Academy, instead of taking four years to graduate high school, I took only two years to complete the program.

I remember Mary Hart, of *Entertainment Tonight*, coaching me in history. When I first came to the academy, we had an American history class together. I did not understand American English because I had learned British English in Kenya. Mary could tell I had some challenges understanding the class. She came to me and said, "Would you mind if you and I set up a time to meet at the library so I can help you with history?"

Mary and her brother, Mike, were in the choir with me, and when school was out we traveled through twelve states singing at churches in the Midwest and on the East Coast.

One evening before choir began, I asked the director, Mr. Madisen, if I could go do my laundry because we were leaving for the tour the following day. Mr. Madisen said to me, "You are pulling my leg." I went and sat down next to Mike. Being naïve as I was, I turned to Mike and asked him why Mr. Madisen had told me I was pulling his leg when I had not touched his leg.

Well, Mike started laughing, and then Mr. Madisen asked him, "What did Nick tell you?"

Mike said, "When Nick asked you if he could go do his laundry, you told him he was pulling your leg. Nick said he did not touch your leg." The whole choir team laughed.

I told the entire choir, "Oh, Americans don't mean what they say."

I had many obstacles in coming to the United States. Getting a passport took two years. Getting a visa took a year. And getting money for airfare took four years. I had doubts sometimes, but I communicated with God more than six times a day. I was in action every day with all these obstacles.

In life, I found out that our future—your future or mine—depends on wanting badly and applying action. We cannot afford to listen to those who are going nowhere in life, who are used to the system of selling their time to make money and the system of home and work until you are seventy-five years old. America belongs to the dreamers who are willing to learn from others and their own experience and take action.

I faced people who advised me but knew nothing about schooling in the United States. They were nice people, but I had to throw away their advice. I learned that the person who has an itchy back is the only one who will scratch it. If you have a purpose or a dream, it is only you who is going to go for it with action—no one else will do it for you.

I heard stories of people who walked six hundred miles from Kenya to Ethiopia to get a passport and visa to come to the United States. Remember that when we face hardship, it causes our minds to solve problems and be different from those who don't have a purpose or dreams. Here is another quotation I found:

> A purpose will cause you to:
> Pray more than the ordinary person,
> Unite more than the ordinary person,
> Risk more than the ordinary person,
> Plan more than the ordinary person,
> Observe more than the ordinary person,
> Sacrifice more than the ordinary person,
> Expect more than the ordinary person.
>
> —Dr. David Livingston

I had the dream and the courage to do whatever it took to come to the United States. Finally, I made it, and I am proud of this country. My final word is, you and I can leave America, but America will never leave us. I have seen many Americans and others who have been educated here leave America, but they still keep it in their thoughts, and they talk about America and how great it is. I am proud to be a part of this country and to call it home.

1

From Kenya to the United States as a Teenager

What I Learned from My Mom

I vividly remember growing up in a hut thatched with grass and pieces of wood. My two sisters and I lived there with our parents, and it did not occur to us that there might be anything better. It was a way of life. We played hide and seek every day, even though there was no place to hide. We were hungry to play, so we created our own fun with excitement. Sometimes we got hurt by the poles around the hut, especially me, as my sisters and I played.

My parents and grandparents had a strong work ethic and respect for elders, and they instilled in us kids a respect for our playmates. The most we wanted was to be at peace with our parents and grandparents, because obedience was very important in those days.

The amazing thing, as I look back, was that we all slept on the floor of the hut, except my dad and mom. They made their own bed with sticks that had strings tied across them. In that hut, we also had calves, goats, sheep, chickens, dogs, and cats. When all the animals urinated on the dirt at night, we slept on that. We didn't know anything better, but I wanted more because I hated that kind of lifestyle. I don't know whether my sisters thought beyond where we were.

One thing I recall was that respect for parents and all people was so important, more than anything else I can remember. We were taught in the villages that if you cannot listen to the teaching and be willing to learn it from your elders, you will be worthless in life. Yes, a few kids deviated from the coaching, and they were cast out by the family. Their lives had no direction.

I had two grandmas. Grandma Mary Kamene was on my dad's side. She was so gracious to all the grandkids, and she always wanted me to pray with her. She was a Salvation Army church member but devoted to salvation for her family. Grandma Miriam Munyiva was on my mom's side. Grandma Miriam was different because whatever she said, she did precisely. She always said I was the most loving grandson, more than all the other grandkids. She and I preached early in the morning on the mountains and prayed together. She was a member of the African Inland Church (AIC). Both grandmas, my mom and dad, and the villagers encouraged me to do the best in life and help others who had a dream or a vision in their lives.

Now I understand the simple teaching I received from my parents, grandparents, and the villagers when they said, "Rain beats a leopard's skin, but it does not wash out the spots." Life can challenge us in so many ways, but it doesn't have to destroy our dreams, our teachings, or our beliefs.

Yes, I have gone through many trials and errors. As I have experienced my life, sometimes it feels as if I have tried everything except leprosy. It is enough to appreciate life and learn more so I can pass it on to others.

The more people we are willing to touch in life, the better off we are in our own lives and the better off we are financially. Life is lived only once. The more we live it with love, the better life gets. We are always finding new friends. I have learned how to expand my friendships instead of criticizing others. Do not judge people; no one who is alive is perfect.

For many years, I tried to find out how poor we were in my family. Sometimes we went without food for as long as four days. From day one, we were taught that "family affairs were not talked about in public squares." In other words, family affairs should not be talked about with just anyone, but only with the people you trust, who are your mentors and who are willing to help you or recommend you to someone else who can help. In the twenty-first century, there is no privacy; we let it out to the public square. Eventually, I came to realize we were so poor that "we spelt poor with five O's." That's very poor. My family never talked about how poor we were but instead lived with hope. The hope was in their children that one day they would grow up and make a difference in their lives and in the lives of others.

Even though we were poor, we kids could tell that our Dad, Mom, and our grandparents on both sides loved us and that nothing could separate us. I also had two grandfathers. My grandpa Mbinda, on my mom's side, was a businessman selling refined African tobacco. I used to go with him to the market fifteen miles away to sell tobacco. My grandpa Tumbo was a storyteller.

Grandpa Tumbo was an amazing man. He got the family together from time to time and spoke his philosophy to the all of us. When Grandpa talked, you could hear a pin drop. There were no interruptions. Grandpa Tumbo was a loving and very hardworking man. He loved his entire family, and the tribe liked him because when the conversation got boring, he made it exciting.

Here is one meaning of the word *proverb*: a proverb is the horse of conversation; when the conversation lags, a proverb will revive it. That was Grandpa Tumbo. He had so much wisdom, more than anyone else I have met. One thing Grandpa Tumbo taught me was to never quit on anything you start as long as it affects people or changes people's lives. Grandpa Tumbo was a man of courage and patience, but he could not stand cowards who surrendered when faced with challenges.

Other grandkids were older than I was and had more advanced reading skills than I had, but every time Grandpa talked I wrote down everything he said. Grandpa Tumbo taught us so much; that is why I am writing this book—to share his wisdom. Grandpa Tumbo taught all his grandkids this: "A roaring lion kills no game." If you have no dreams or passion, or you are not willing to go after your dreams with passion, it is all just talk.

Grandpa's belief was that no matter what we were going through, we should always be learning. Why did I pay attention to Grandpa? Was I an amazing grandkid? Indeed, I was not, but I think I had a vision to serve others, and I did not care about the cost. Here is something Grandpa Tumbo said over and over, and I will never forget it: "One cannot both feast and become rich." We have to be committed to something and pursue it until we achieve it.

Grandpa, with two hundred grandkids, said so many times, "The cricket cries all the year around, but the year changes." I have heard this saying more than two thousand times: "I will do this and that when things get better." What is important is to have a purpose or a dream and to think of it every day. This is why so many people waste their valuable lives waiting. Without a dream, they end up with a job starting from the bottom and end up at the bottom financially. Dream big.

I spent so much time with my grandpa Tumbo, and I am so glad I did. Here is my conclusion about Grandpa Tumbo—he was a man of integrity and an open-minded man. He taught all his grandkids the proverb that "he who lives with an ass, makes noises like an ass." It is so amazing that in America 95 percent of people believe that a job will bring financial freedom. Here is the sad thing—that we foreigners are getting rich and people born in this country are going backward. Why? Grandpa Tumbo told us that "a single stick may smoke but will not burn."

My grandpa Tumbo taught us that "to be without a friend is to be poor, indeed." Let's create friends and love them.

Grandpa Tumbo was a man of gracious integrity and action. Let's be truthful in life. Let me be precise from my grandpa Tumbo on what he taught us: "Two eyes see better than one eye."

Finally, Grandpa taught us this: "Good millet is known at the harvest."

A great gift I inherited from my parents was something my grandpa taught us, and that is, "Let your love be like the misty rain, coming softly but flooding the river." What Grandpa meant was to love and not look for any credit or appraisal from anyone, but to count it in your heart and continue doing so until you reach a few who are willing to change the world. Any one of us can change the world if we have a dream and want it badly enough to learn and take action for our purpose every day. Mom and Dad did not know how to read or write, but they learned through their parents' beliefs and philosophy. They were taught not to just settle for anything but to believe you can be anything you want to be, if you choose to be and you are hungry for it.

Our gracious mom had great wisdom from her mom, Miriam, who was a strong believer. Mom watched over us kids in the evenings, and she knew we were hungry. Grandma Miriam taught her how to comfort us during times of hunger or in any bad situation. If we did not go to bed, she told us that if we went to sleep we would not be hungry anymore.

I also learned from this that people who are hungry stay up late, and the ones who are not hungry go to sleep. In life, if you are hungry you will be up in action, and if you are not hungry you will go to sleep and do nothing. In my experience, the people who make a difference in other people's lives are hungry and active.

Be hungry and go for actions, and fear will lessen. Why do I say this? My grandpa said it better than I: "Wood already touched by the fire is not hard to set alight." If you have a purpose with action, it's not hard to see the results. Action is the key to getting what you want in life. When you have the hunger, you go after what you want.

Grandpa said, "A man with too much ambition cannot sleep in peace." If we are hungry, we are going to be in action with fear or without fear. I have been hungry, and I know that when you are hungry, you can do anything. Hunger creates actions.

Here is the point I want to make for you and me. When I decided with hunger to come to the United States, several other people I knew were also trying to come to this country. All of them told me I was nothing and that I would not make it to the United States. I almost accepted their words, but in the end I refused their discouragement. These were good friends, and they loved me, but they were like 95 percent of the population who are content to get a job, start on a low level, and end up on a lower level. Being poor is temporary if we have the dream and go after it with hard work and pain. Even though I was very poor in my childhood, I believed that when I grew up I would never be poor.

Sometimes when I hear people say they grew up poor in America, I wonder how poor. They have shelter, food, a TV, a car, clothes, schools, and toilet paper. We had none of these in my dad's house. We had nothing, and I came out of that. This is why I am writing about struggles.

We go through a life of struggle. But if you have a purpose, if you forge ahead to dream about it and act to do something about it, the rain may beat on you, but it will not wash out your spots.

Starting School

When I was growing up, there was no law in Kenya that children had to go to school. I have no idea where my parents learned that education was important. They had no formal education themselves.

One day, my parents told me that I was going to school. It was a totally different language for me, and I had no idea what they were talking about. My duty every day was to look after the cattle, and I loved it.

Before enrolling in the first grade, I was taking care of more than two thousand cattle. My job was to take them grazing and to the rivers to drink. They followed behind the ox I rode. In those days, the men used to train cattle to follow a bell by having someone lead them ringing the bell and someone behind the cattle directing them to follow the bell man. It took six months to train them. Before I could watch over the cattle, I also had to be trained by Grandpa, Dad, my uncle, and one of my cousins.

We had to be trained at a young age on how to fight anything that attacked livestock. We had bows and arrows and sharp swords to carry with us, but there were a lot of snakes and other dangerous animals. It was not an easy thing. Grandfathers and dads had to find the child who was the risk taker for this job. I have been a risk taker all my life. We also had to learn each animal's character by watching it and talking to the animal. If any cattle got lost, it was a problem because the elders had to go look for it. Every evening, when Grandpa was telling stories at the cows' gate, I was praised by my grandpa and my dad. At six years old, I was responsible to do everything the family wanted me to do. I was very young.

My sister Phyllis was older than I, and she knew what our parents meant when they talked about school. When the day came to start, we began our journey in the early morning. My sister held my hand. We walked eight miles each way, wearing only our khaki school uniforms. In those days there wasn't any boarding, so we had to go back and forth each day between school and home. Today I appreciate how hardship brings rewards because my parents did not accept excuses. Grandpa used to say, "Don't ask what is being born. You will see the child."

We walked to school eight miles one way, and we were treated as responsible kids by our parents. Education was second to none in those days. We went to school early in the morning and laughed and played with each other along the way. We told stories and created fun and excitement. Every story had life meaning. In school, we played soccer, which we called football, and ran all sorts of track events.

My sister and I would wake up at five in the morning to get ready for school. No food, no shoes, no underwear, but a khaki school uniform that we were required to wear every day. Even though we went so often without food and clothes and many basic needs, our teaching that "family affairs were not discussed in public squares" meant we could not tell other students, teachers, or anyone that we had not had food for days.

My sister and I learned teamwork. After school, at three o'clock, we knew that when we got home there would be no food, so we found and ate wild fruits on the way home. We ate evening to evening, if we were lucky. We learned to eat the wild fruits to survive, and we learned to eat the ones that were safe. I don't know how we learned, but we were very careful.

From first grade to fourth grade we walked back and forth each day, eight miles one way.

My sister and I got to school on our first day, and I panicked. There were so many kids, more than God had created, and I was the youngest. The first few months at school I hated it. I came to know there was a campaign for all kids to go to school. I kept a list of all the names of the kids from my village who went to school at the same time I did. I was very accurate because I knew them all, even though I was so young. From first grade, I went to school with twenty kids from my village. I was a loner, and I am an independent thinker even today. I was really too young for school those days. We had no preschool as they do today, and the first year of going to school was hard for me. I repeated first grade, and all of the other twenty kids moved to second grade.

It did not disappoint me going through first grade twice. Most of the kids really loved me, and when they saw me repeating first grade, they were surprised that I was not smart. Grandpa used to say, "To try and fail is not laziness." I did all I could my first year in school, but I was too young to grasp it. Yes, I went through first grade twice, but from there I got all the basics, and I outran every student in the school by achieving the highest grades. "Good millet is known at the harvest."

The second year, I was still walking eight miles to school with my sister and other kids from my village. The only clothes we had were the school uniforms. Most of the kids we went to school with had parents who were a little better off than we were, but my vision was that one day I would be wealthy.

As my grandpa said, "Let your love be like the misty rain, coming softly but flooding the river." All my sister and I had was love and encouragement from our parents and both sets of grandparents. We got unconditional love from them in spite of whatever happened in our education.

"If relatives help each other, what evil can hurt them?"

In those days, the grades were called Standard One, Two, Three, and Four. The situation was that we had to pay school fees or we were kicked out. I had a dream that I had to do whatever it took to get an education. I remember Grandpa saying, "Unless you call out, who will open the door?" As poor as my parents were, I had to think of a way to earn money to go to school. Indeed, to be so poor that you spell "poor" with five O's is no fun.

Grandpa Tumbo said, "He who conceals his disease cannot expect to be cured."

Note this precisely, "Talking with one another is loving one another." He who learns, teaches. I decided to go to my uncle and ask him if I could work for him looking after livestock for pay. All my life, I have made decisions and acted on them; otherwise, "the fool is thirsty in the midst of water." My gracious uncle, when I asked to work for him on Fridays, Saturdays, and Sundays so I could pay my school fees, said, "Yes. You can work looking after the cattle, goats, and sheep."

As soon as I asked him, I kept silent. Note my grandpa's outstanding statement, "The fool speaks; the wise man listens." My uncle said yes, I could look after his livestock, and he would pay me ten shillings per month. In American money, that is only $1.50 per month. To many people, that sounds like too little, but in Kenya in those days it was a lot of money. Every time he paid me, I paid the school fees and gave the rest to my mom.

In first grade I started working for my uncle. I paid my own tuition for four years, from first grade through fourth grade. My parents had to pay school fees for my sister.

"Not all the flowers of a tree produce flowers." Not all the kids of the same parents have a productive life. My brothers and sisters produced different results even though we came from the same parents. They produced as much as their dreams could give them with their hard work.

The money I earned from my uncle paid my school fees and fed my family. When my parents did not have enough money to pay my sister's fees, they used my money to pay for her, as well. My only thinking was, "If one person can do it, another person can do it."

After one year of working for my uncle, the second year I had no work. I recall Grandpa saying, "He who is being carried on someone's back does not realize how far the town is." If we are supported by someone, we become so comfortable we have no plans or goals. After I stopped working for my uncle, I had to find other ways to generate income. The job ended when I was in second grade, so I worked for other people over the weekends—building trenches for their farms to keep the rain from washing out the soil. I was taught young how to solve problems on my own, and if I could not solve the problems, I had to seek mentorship from my dad or grandpa.

I had a cousin who never liked school, and he lived at our home. He saw the struggle we were going through without food, clothes, and so many things. Grandpa used to say, "There is no one who lives with a person who has smallpox and fails to get smallpox."

My cousin told me that we should escape or run away to go to work to feed the family. Well, I had to listen to him; he was older than I. He was in fourth grade, while I was now only in third. One day we got out of school and threw all our books away. We decided we were going to go to work in a place called Konza, thirty miles away from home. We walked and ran to get there through the national parks, where there were dangerous animals. We walked among the lions, leopards, elephants, you name it. My cousin had done it before, so he knew how to avoid danger. I learned how to avoid being attacked by those animals by not looking at them but walking straight. I think it is by the grace of God that both my cousin and I are still alive. Many others have been killed by lions or leopards walking the same route we took through this region of dangerous animals.

I had never walked thirty miles before, but I did it with my cousin. I would guess it took us fifteen hours to reach Konza.

When you are hungry, nothing is difficult. My cousin and I started working for Indians who had recently arrived from India. I had never cooked in my life, but if you want something badly enough and are willing to learn, you can do anything. In two days, I learned how to make Indian food.

I don't know where I learned that "ignorance has no defense." I never knew how to wash clothes, and all I had to wear was my khaki school uniform. Cooking and doing everyday work for two months, my uniform became dirty and black from the wood charcoal. I never washed it. It was stinking, and people could smell it from eight yards away.

Remember, when you have a dream, passion, or vision, you go for it without caring what anyone thinks about you. You are doing it for you, period, and you don't have to pay attention to the ones who want to give advice and have nothing of their own to show for it. Decide and act.

After my cousin and I had worked for three months, we decided to go back home to feed the family. We had saved everything we earned because we had no living expenses at all. We walked again thirty miles. When we got home, all our parents had was thanks that we had returned safely. Think big and act on any situation.

We both missed school for three months. Do you think anyone cared where we were? No, but our parents worried about us the whole time.

We returned to school, and one day it hit me hard that I had to be different in my thinking than the other kids. I started thinking that I had a chance to do better in life, and life changed.

I said to myself, *if I keep on running away from school, I will be like all the other kids in my village, be into drugs, do nothing, and make no progress at all.* I made up my mind not to be with my cousin anymore.

The next time my cousin asked me to escape from school and go to work again, I told him that I was going to school with no more escaping. Our relationship ended there, and we are separated even to this day.

Grandpa, with his belief, said it in a proper way, "A man who has been tossed by a buffalo, when he sees a black ox, thinks it is another buffalo." If you have failed, when you see another opportunity, you think about failure. Or, if you have seen an opportunity and succeeded, when you see another opportunity, you think of success. If we live with parents who work for someone else all their lives, that's all we think of in life—going back and forth between home and work for forty-five to fifty-five years. We get hired for a low-level job, and after many years of work we end up on a lower level.

I told my cousin no. Today my cousin is nothing but a wisher. Don't let your present life be wasted by fear or by listening to the wrong people. I'm in the United States today as a citizen because I acted on my dreams, even when I faced so many discouragements, more than anyone I can think of. Decide and make changes for a better life.

I have found that when we have hunger, we feel the pressure to find other people who also have dreams. As my grandpa Tumbo told us grandkids, "No one lives with someone who has smallpox and fails to get smallpox." I decided to split from my cousin and pursue my education.

The interesting thing is that when I started first grade there were twenty kids from our village. By the end of four years, all the other kids had dropped out of school, even my sister Phyllis. I was left alone walking eight miles one way, crossing rivers and going through hilly places all by myself. I had a dream not to quit. Really, quitting is nothing but surrendering to failure.

All I had was hunger for education and nothing less than that. I paid attention to Grandpa's philosophy and belief because he had wisdom. Grandpa said, "When a needle falls into a deep well, many people will look into the well, but few will be ready to go down after it."

We hear people say, "I want to do this and that," but what they lack is a dream or hunger. You've got to want it so badly that you eat it, sleep it, and think about it every day. It doesn't matter what you want to do, but you have to want it so badly that you get it in spite of anything. If you are going to achieve, and you want to so badly, I believe that God will support you as long as you act. Action cures fear. Do you really want it badly?

Looking After Livestock

One thing I knew was that I did not have decayed dreams. But there is no cure that does not cost. Sometimes over the weekends, I had to do other chores from six to ten in the morning before I could go to look after the livestock on the mountains.

Because my uncle accepted me to work for him, he had to coach me on several things about looking after livestock:

1. I could not fall asleep because snakes could bite me, and I would die.
2. I could not fall asleep because goats and sheep could be killed and eaten by wildlife.
3. I had to follow instructions.

Each Friday, Saturday, and Sunday I walked a mile to my uncle's place. First thing when I got there, I had to open the barn door. Then I had to untie the goats and sheep from their ropes. In the barn in the evenings, the goats and sheep were each tied with rope on one front leg. We always had to make sure the ropes were not too tight, because they could cause a wound. If a too-tight rope caused a wound and the animal could not keep up with the others, then we had to kill it for food.

After untying the ropes, the goats and sheep formed a line coming out from the barn. As they lined up, they waited for me to lead them to where they were supposed to graze. Mind you, I was trained at a young age to train animals. They did not run at all but stayed in a line and waited until I was ready to lead them to where they were bound to graze all day. I did not worry about them as long as I could see every animal. If one animal was not with the crowd, then I had to worry about it, and I had to find it. In many cases, the animal was resting.

The next thing I had to do was open the gate for the cattle. The cattle gate was close to the hut we lived in—about twenty yards away. The gate was made of wood crossing bars, and opening this gate we had to take one piece at a time and pile the gate bars aside.

My uncle had about twenty goats, fifteen sheep, and fifty cows. My grandpa had more than two hundred cattle and a lot of goats and sheep. I had to graze all the animals from nine in the morning to seven in the evening. I had to gather the cattle, goats, and sheep to drink water from the river at noon. We did not have clocks, but sometimes we would hear a rooster, donkey, or certain birds make noise, or we would watch the sun. Mind you, the sun set by four o'clock because there were many mountains.

During the rainy season, it was fun taking livestock to drink water from the river close to home. But during a drought, we had to take them to the river about five to seven miles away. We could not use shortcuts because people who owned the land in between did not want livestock going across it. Cattle, goats, and sheep that crossed a piece of land during drought tended to destroy it.

I had a brown cane of wood that I had made myself. The cane was to hit the rocks to talk to any animal that did not stay together with the others. The animals understood what I was saying because they came to join the herd.

It was important to watch for dangerous wild animals, such as hyenas, foxes, and leopards, so they wouldn't eat the goats and sheep. I had a dog with me, and it was trained to protect the animals. I was lucky that I never lost any of the goats and sheep.

The villages were all in the foothills. When you watch animals all the time, you are constantly moving because the animals are always moving. It was important not to sleep when watching livestock. Also, if you fell asleep, you could endanger your life by getting bitten by snakes or other dangerous animals.

Sometimes I wonder, *why did I do all this as a young boy?* I am comforted by recalling Grandpa saying, "He who does not cultivate his field will die of hunger." I had to do whatever it took to earn money to pay for my tuition and to feed my family. There was no free lunch. You never heard anyone in those days say, "Oh, I'm tired." That was construed as a voice of laziness.

Let me open up your mind by telling you that, as young as I was, I looked after livestock for Dad, Uncle, Uncle, and Uncle. Papa Tumbo said, "Good millet is known at the harvest." Be a producer, a worker, and a driver, and you will see the world better.

I was busy and alert looking after livestock all day. Then during the evening, from ten o'clock to midnight, sometimes we kids played outside. We had no electricity, so we played in total darkness. The beauty was to play in the dark and look up at the stars. They always looked so precious to us. Sometimes we could walk at night, with no moon or stars, and not get off the path. The only thing we had to be aware of was by luck not to step on snakes. We liked to play at night, and we had to respect one another. We had to love one another. All these things we were taught at a very young age. Papa always said, "Love is like a baby. It needs to be treated tenderly."

In June and July it gets cold, as low as forty-five degrees. During these months, I used to make fires to warm up. As the animals moved around, I made other fires. Before the day was over, I would have made six fires. Because we had no matches, I created fire with two sticks by spinning them on each other until a fire got started. Before I left each fire, I had to start another fire, and after it got started, I came back to put out the first one. I was all alone with the animals. Most of the time I whistled, and that was a sign of joy. Sometimes I would sing aloud, songs like "Nearer My God to Thee, Nearer to Thee."

Another thing I learned looking after livestock was to shoot with a bow and poison arrows. I took my bow and arrows with me all the time, but I had days when my intuition told me I would need them.

The arrows were made from bamboo and certain trees. If you have seen arrows, their construction looks pretty much the same around the world. The difference with the arrows we used was at the back, where you pull to let them go. Ours had three cut wings from the rooster. They were glued in so that when the arrow was shot it would travel far away. It looked like the wings of a plane. Also, the arrows had sharpened metal tips that I made myself.

The poison was made up of the smoke from the huts we lived in, and we added other poisons from wild plants. If you shot an animal with an arrow, it took ten to twenty minutes for the animal to die. When we had tribal fighting, my tribe, the Kamba, used poisonous arrows, and the Masai used spears.

If you were looking after livestock, it was important to have your bow and arrows with you because you could not tell when a dangerous wild animal could attack the livestock. I always had my stick and my bow and arrows. I was brought up to fight anything that attacked me or my family.

Looking after livestock sounds like an easy thing, but it is not, because you have to be obedient and ambitious, and also a fast runner. I was all of those things.

During the summer, when it was hot and we had no rain for a while, I had to climb tall trees to find shelter. When I climbed, I had to sit down and not fall asleep. Up in the tree, I could watch cattle, goats, and sheep and also animals that attacked livestock.

My uncle sometimes had the authority to tell my parents whether I was a good shepherd. Well, Grandpa Tumbo made this statement when all of us grandkids sat down at the cattle gate. He said, "Don't call the forest that shelters you a jungle." This means do not blame or gossip about the company for which you work unless you have an alternative. From my life experience, the world will give you and me what we allow it to give us. You and I will change the world or leave it the way we found it.

I am telling my life story, but I have done everything in life with no education and with education. I have worked for more than thirty-four corporations and governments. It is accurate to say that the corporate world is so sick that it doesn't care about you at all but their philosophy is lets pay you little as much they can.

Looking after livestock is not all that different from working in the corporate world. If we don't control our financial freedom, we will never be financially free. I came to the United States as a teenager with forty-five dollars. I am not better than anyone else, but I don't like the phrase "I will try," because "try" indicates failure with no commitment. Someone said, "Disabled minds look for security in a job and will never find it." The corporate world is all about "doing it to others before they do it to you."

How People Survived in the Village

"He who cannot dance will say, 'The drum is bad.'"

When I was growing up, I observed many things in my village. When we had plenty of rain and people harvested plenty of food that season, some people did not consider that one day we would have drought again. People did not think about drought, and they sold most of their food at harvest and ate the rest. So when drought came again, they had no food. "Unless you call out, who will open the door?" These people had to go to their neighbors and get some food to feed their families. Seeing is different from being told. As a young boy, I saw all this in real life.

"The one-eyed man thanks God only when he sees a man who is totally blind." I used to think, *why do we have to go through four days without any food?* until I saw kids who were dying from hunger.

"To spend the night in anger is better than spending it in repentance." Going through all this I never got angry with my parents at all.

During good times, we had plenty to eat, such as greens, vegetables, beans, corn, and a lot of fruits. In many cases, as livestock got older the elders killed it and shared the meat with the villagers and neighbors. There was a lot of sharing.

Sharing was big in the village. If you were eating by yourself while others were around and you did not offer them food, you were considered a selfish person. The tradition was that if you were hungry, you could stop at the village in any house without anyone home. You could eat, but you couldn't take any food with you. If you took food with you, you were construed as a thief. If identified as a thief, you were an enemy in the village and an outcast. To be obedient in this and other rules was very important. All obedient children were given more chores to do and disobedients were given less chores, because there was less trust on them.

During good years when we had plenty of food, the villagers shared with other villagers what they grew. They exchanged food, whatever it was. The elders worshipped a lot, thanking their god for blessings. The elders got together in the evenings and drank native beer, and each one spoke to his or her god. All you could hear was the response of men and calmness of appreciation to God for plenty of food.

The old African slavery time said, "Ivory first, then your baby." The villagers believed that the first priority was to feed your family, and other things were secondary.

During drought, people had to deal with it, but it taught people how to survive and stay strong believing rain would come. The villagers did not move; there was no place to move to. Some distant shops were about ten miles' walk one way. Sometimes you would go to buy corn or beans to bring to your family, and when you arrived there would be no food to buy. When you left to buy food, people hoped that you would bring food home with you. If the shops had no food, then parents had to go around the village searching out who had corn and beans. Sometimes some villagers did not like other villagers. Grandpa said it properly, and this applies to individuals or cultures: "Don't try to make someone hate the person he loves, for he will still go on loving, but he will hate you."

Children at Play

An African proverb says, "When you follow in the path of your father, you learn to walk like him." The first thing every child in the village had to learn was to be creative and to relate with other good children with good discipline. Remember, my grandpa always told all his grandchildren, "No one lives with someone with smallpox and fails to get smallpox." The meaning is this: if we hang around with those who do bad things, we will be influenced by their behavior to also do bad things. Children had to learn to serve others and expect no recognition.

We had no technology, so we had to create our own entertainment. Here is how we managed to create our playthings:

1. We made our own toy cars and planes from wood.
2. We made roller skates from wood.
3. We made ropes for jumping on from sisal fiber. We had a lot of fun jumping from them.
4. We made anything we wanted from clay.
5. We climbed on trees.
6. We played with rhinos by chasing them, and they chased us, and we had to know how to climb trees very quickly. If you were not faster, you were dead. We had learned a long time ago that rhinos could only see twenty feet away. I and other kids from my village, we are alive today by the grace of God. All the kids were taught not to cry at all. We were taught that crying men are weak and cannot protect the family.
7. We made slings. These were to kill birds, rabbits, and other small animals.

Everything we made as children, we did by watching others do it; then we would practice. We had to be creative to stay happy and busy. Laziness was not accepted by the culture. If you were lazy, you had a hard time finding someone to marry you, and marriage was very important in those days.

When we were growing up, we were taught that boys and girls should play separately. In the evening when the stars were out, all the kids played together. We played for many hours at night, and we laughed all the time.

When I was growing up, discipline was essential for all the kids. Here is another African proverb: "If your son laughs when you scold him, you ought to cry, for you have lost him; if he cries, you may laugh, for you have a worthy heir."

My dad was so humble but had a big heart for people. The only thing my dad and I totally disagreed on was his relatives taking land and things from him. For me, I would have been dead fighting with bows and arrows.

Here is an African proverb: "The heart of a wise man lies quiet like limpid water." In life, be nice to all people. We all face challenges and disappointments. Indeed, Grandpa said properly that "those who are absent are always wrong." I claim this teaching because I have done it myself, and it never worked at all. An African proverb rightly says that "a single stick may smoke, but it will not burn." If all we want is to win and be happy, then we need to value others in their games in life. Our game in life is how you and I learn to play it. "The opportunity that God sends does not wake up those who are asleep." All I can say is that I have done everything in life, so that all that remains is completion.

Men and Women

"To be without a friend is to be poor indeed."

The days when we were growing up were totally different than today. During the day, the men went to plow the farms with oxen. Sometimes, if there was nothing to do, the men made beer from sugar cane and drank together and told stories. Sometimes they talked in proverbs, because proverbs are the "daughters of experience." Sometimes they talked about beautiful women. Men believed in those days that "he who marries a beauty marries trouble." Also, men believed that "a wise man who knows proverbs can reconcile difficulties."

In the evenings, the men got together with Grandpa and all the boys and made a fire close to the cows' gate to tell stories as men only. Grandpa Tumbo was a tall man, and we carried him when he could not walk, but he had such a brilliant mind. I loved to sit outside each evening at the cows' gate with the fire.

Each evening, Grandpa would repeat to two hundred grandkids and their dads his philosophy that "wood already touched by the fire is not hard to set alight." Grandpa was not educated and did not know how to read or write. Grandpa Tumbo said over and over, "One cannot both feast and become rich." We have to be committed to something and pursue it until we achieve it. We are in the twenty-first century, and Grandpa's philosophy is still applicable today.

The big thing both men and women believed was that preparing their children to face life was the best they could give.

In the evenings, Grandma, Mom, and the girls sat in the hut cooking and teaching the girls how to be good women by being obedient.

Women did harder work than the men. During the day, women had to get firewood, whether it was a short distance or a long distance away. They would pile twenty to forty pounds of wood, tie it with rope, and carry it on their backs. I did it helping my mom, and it was not an easy job. They milked the cows, and so did I. Another hard job they did was cultivating the farms when the crops were growing. Men were not supposed to do women's jobs, but I did some of them, and that's why Mom used to tell people, "When Mutiso dies, his coffin will be running." Mutiso is my middle name, and it means "I was born when it was lightning."

The women cultivated and harvested large fields, ten acres plus. They used swords to harvest all the crops and put them in bags made of sisal fiber. These bags could carry more than fifty or sixty pounds.

The most amazing part of farming was after the crops were planted and had started to grow. Then came the cultivation of the crops, keeping the weeds from growing around the corn or the beans.

When a family in the village had a big farm, as my parents had, the woman would invite all the women in the village and the neighboring villages to come together and cultivate certain farms together. Women loved working together even if they had to walk quite a distance. Here is the amazing thing. All the women would dress up with brightly colored clothes and ornaments, such as beads, necklaces, and metal on their ankles that made noise. This is unexplainable in words. All these women prepared for that day of going to cultivate the crops, and they made it fun.

They would do the cultivating in lines with a simple tool, and while they were doing it, they would sing, whistle, and shake their shoulders with all the metal ornaments making noise. They did that all day as a team with joy and fun. I used to watch them, and they instilled in me a joy of life. Indeed, cultivating crops is not easy work.

The person who invited these gracious women to cultivate the crops had to make food and bring it to the farm. I watched this many times because I like to study things and people as I talk to them. These women really had a commitment, which I call "do good and leave behind a virtue that the storm of time can never destroy."

These women, when they were eating food and taking a break from their work, had one person at a time talk about the joy of cultivating the crops. Here is the amazing thing: you could hear a pin drop. They listened and nodded their heads, and all you could hear from them was a response of "mmm-mm" all the way through. None of these women knew how to read or write, but they listened without interruption. When women were cultivating the crops and eating together, the tradition was that no man could come close or interrupt. If a man did, he would not have any respect in the village. In other words, because that man had no respect for women, he would be included in a coward list, and during the tribal wars that man was excluded from protecting the women.

When you listened to these women sing, the songs touched your heart. After they all finished eating, they took what was left to their homes.

Men and women did not choose whom they were going to marry in those days, but the marriage and engagement were announced by the men on both sides of the bride's and groom's families.

A woman had no clue when she would be married. The groom decided when it was time to go get her. When he was ready, he found three or four men to go and get her. One person that day had to watch the bride's movements.

As long as she was not at her parents' home, they could get her anywhere she was that day.

When the men on the bride's and groom's sides agreed, the marriage was a done deal. The tradition was that both the groom and bride had to come from good families. The villagers observed the character of each family. According to my grandparents, marriage was more than four legs in a bed. In those days divorce was rare.

Mighty Young Kids Working

Papa said this one day when we were sitting at the cows' gate, and I wrote it down: "When the bee comes to your house, let her have a beer; you may want to visit the bee's house someday."

I don't recall many kids in my village, Nzaini, who worked at my age. According to our gracious grandpa's belief, here is what happened in my case. When I started school, everyone said I could not make it in school except my gracious parents and all my grandparents. They knew me very well, and they knew I could do anything I wanted to do.

Even though my parents and grandparents disagreed with the village underestimating me, they did not talk about it because my grandpa Tumbo's belief was, "If two horses fight, the grass under their hooves will suffer." This means no one wins in any argument. With all the villagers believing I wouldn't make it in school, Dad and Mom would say, "Let's wait and see."

One time I was kicked out of school because I had no money to pay the fees, and my dad tried to borrow money from my uncles. He took me with him, but the words they told my dad were not words you and I want to hear. Here is Papa's philosophy: "A cutting word is worse than a bowstring; a cut may heal, but the cut of the tongue does not." I decided to work at an early age because of what I listened to. I did not like the words my uncles said to my dad, but they inspired me to be different, to be the best I could. I remember going to my dad and telling him, "Dad, I will do my best in life, and I will help you and Mom." That I did, faithfully supporting them. Eventually, I built them a house of seven bedrooms and bought a farm for them. When you face challenges, you either change with action or live with ifs and buts. When you face challenges, stay in action solving the challenge.

We walked to school eight miles one way, and we were treated as responsible adults by our parents. Papa said, "If relatives help each other, what evil can hurt them?" The idea of having many kids was that the kids would help with farming, looking after livestock, and doing many chores. Children were wealth because the more you had, the more help you got.

An African proverb says, "One finger alone cannot kill lice or flies." No one can accomplish anything worthwhile by himself or herself. So you want to accomplish more in life? Then involve others who want to get involved in touching others. Get to know people and find something you like about them.

In the village where I grew up, there were a lot of encouragements, even though we had challenges with family who did not have a purpose like those who had more dreams to advance. In my case, my dad lost a farm, taken by his stepbrother, who was a chief. One day I got upset, and I got a bow and arrows to go kill the chief. My dear mom had to shout to me not to do it. She and Grandma sat down with me, telling me not to do it. African culture was all about family, and young ones were coached to respect their parents and their elders.

One thing I appreciated growing up was sitting down with my gracious grandpas in the evening telling stories. It's where I learned about loving. Indeed, I have accepted what Papa Tumbo said: "Let your love be like the misty rain, coming softly but flooding the river."

I am in America today because of my purpose to start the struggle to come to the United States at a young age. I found that when you have a purpose, when you are willing to work, when you have a mentor, and when you are open to listening, you will do well spiritually and in touching others because you have a cause. Get a cause and be willing to work for your purposes.

One day I was looking after cattle for our family and another uncle. We had a serious famine that year, and I'd had no food for two days. I had learned all by myself to look for food for survival while looking after the livestock.

There was a huge, tall tree close to the banks of the river. None of the kids from my village ever wanted to climb this tree because if you fell down thirty feet, you were dead. That day I was hungry and sad. "If the heart is sad, tears will follow." I decided to climb this tall tree. No one was close by. I climbed the tree way up, about twenty feet. I rested on one of the branches, eating the sweet wild fruits.

When I decided to come down, I started losing my balance because I was sliding down too quickly. I was lucky and caught a branch, and I hung on it for ten minutes crying and screaming. Grandpa said, "Unless you call out, who will open the door?"

Screaming and crying helped because one of the village kids that afternoon was coming home from school. He heard the crying and screaming. He saw me hanging on the branch of that tree. This village kid knew I was in danger of falling and dying. Although many kids feared climbing that tree, this village kid climbed it within a short time and grabbed me down from that branch. I was shaking and crying. "Sitting doing nothing is being crippled."

The Power of One

When I was growing up in my village, you were rich if you had a lot of cattle, goats, and sheep. Grandpa had many cattle. As the years went by, however, the grass on our land began disappearing because of drought.

There was a new development more than a hundred miles away called Makueni. It was new land, but jungle. A lot of mosquitoes lived there. It was free land for anyone who wanted to risk his life by dying from malaria. One day the elders decided to select kids who were obedient and good at looking after livestock to take a herd of cattle there because of the famine. They picked several kids, and my mom found out I was one of those to go. "He may say he loves you; wait and see what he does for you."

My gracious mom spoke to the elders and told them that her son was not going to die, but she would rather die for him. The tradition was different because women had no power to say anything. She told her dad, my grandpa. He was strong, and he did not play around. Grandpa told the elders that his daughter was right, and her son was more important to her than her life. He was behind my mom about me not going to die. The village elders surrendered, and I was free from going to the land of death.

All the kids who were selected walked a hundred miles and took cows there. Mom was right; none of the kids came back. All of them died from malaria. My mom was a friend, and I recall Papa Mbinda, Mom's dad, telling us, "To be without a friend is to be poor indeed."

I am here today because my mom heard a voice from God to speak up about me not going to die from malaria. This was tough for her in those days. Every person in the village turned against my mom. I was very young, but my faith was to pray for her. My faith in God has been strong all my life.

Grandpa Mbinda said so many times, "A word uttered cannot be taken back." Mom spoke what she spoke, and she could not take it back because she loved me enough to fight the right fight.

"Rain beats a leopard's skin, but it does not wash out the spots."

Yes, during those days when Mom defended me from putting my life in danger, so many bad things were said about her by the elders. She kept her attitude cool. Here I am today because of her, and those elders had disabled minds because they did not have a vision as my gracious mom had. Don't be afraid to speak your thoughts, even if there is danger. The power of one woman changed the entire village after they saw her truth of all the kids dying from malaria who had gone away to look after cattle.

The power of one is helping other people. The power of one is loving many people unconditionally. The power of one is overcoming any obstacles.

The power of one is praying for other people and serving them with your given gifts.

The power of one is to see an opportunity to make money and help the ones who want so much to achieve it.

Examination after Four Years

At the end of fourth grade we had to take a final exam to go on to fifth grade and intermediate school. Not many schools in those days had fifth to eighth grade. An attitude of discouragement is expensive. Within the first four years, most of the students—more than three-quarters of them—quit school. I continued going to school—the only one from my village.

During fourth grade, we had to walk twelve miles to take the exams to qualify for intermediate school. Stop thinking about problems, but handle them. I ate at home and walked twelve miles to take the exam for two days. For two days I had no food. I was hungry. After we completed the exams, I walked home—again twelve miles.

The first time I took these exams, I failed. Only two people qualified from my school. Don't surrender on anything if you have a dream to accomplish. I repeated fourth grade. I was not disappointed, but I had to find a new dream and set up a different goal for my action. If there is no action, expect zero results. The second time I took the exams to qualify for fifth grade, I was one of seventeen out of forty-five students who qualified from my school. Purpose with actions will change you.

In those days, not many schools had fifth through eighth grade; I would say not more than thirty in all of Kenya. There were not more than ten high schools in the entire country. There were more students than the schools could accommodate. We all ended up going to different schools. Some students went to school a hundred miles away from their homes, and some went to school ten to twenty miles one way. This may not sound like a big deal, but in those days it was a big deal. For me, the distance from my village to the school was not such a big deal because we were all used to walking each day.

"Cross the river in a crowd and the crocodile won't eat you." After all twenty students from my village quit school, all I had was a hunger for education and faith in God, and nothing else. Pursue your passion and God will be with you, but act on what you want. The truth is, without action nothing will change in your life or mine. The twenty students from my village helped me develop more desire for competition. Nothing comes from nothing. We have to work to achieve our purpose.

"A cow with no tail should not chase flies." It was Grandpa Tumbo's philosophy. What it means is that if you have no dreams, you will never pursue them.

From fifth grade to eighth grade, I walked over the mountains barefoot in a khaki uniform twelve miles one way. I left home at three in the morning to get to school at seven. Indeed, we get nothing for nothing. We have to earn it.

Grandpa said, "A man who has been tossed by a buffalo, when he sees a black ox thinks it is another buffalo." He meant that if you have a bad experience or failure, when you see an opportunity, you think it is another failure.

My concern with going to fifth grade and beyond was how I was going to pay for tuition. I knew that I could not work and go to school. I had to talk to Mom and Dad about my school fees. Mom was a go-getter person. She said it was up to her and my dad to pay my tuition now, and she added, "We will do whatever it takes." Mom was the driver in our family, and she was results oriented, so I depended on her 100 percent. Dad was a detail person. I used to tell Dad, "I'll bet you even know when a fly dies."

Grandpa said, "Love is like young rice—transplanted, still it grows."

My parents were the most loving people I ever knew. They wanted me to succeed so I could do more financially and teach others about life and its challenges.

Grandpa said, "A cutting word is worse than a bowstring; a cut may heal, but the cut of the tongue does not." My parents had only encouragements for me.

In fifth grade, I was kicked out of school for not paying tuition and also for not obeying the colonial British rules. Even then, my parents were aware of their duty or responsibility to put me through school.

Here is more from Grandpa: "The cow steps on the calf, but she does not hate it." And, "It's better to be loved than feared." You can discipline your kids, but you still love them.

I ran into a lot of challenges from fifth to eighth grade because I could not stand the British rule in Kenya and their authority over everything. Sometimes I was suspended from school because I hated the song "God Bless the Queen." I hated to say sir or madam. My dad had to discipline me on British rule, but I rejected it. My dad still loved me.

Without work or money from my uncle, hard times came up. We could not afford to pay school fees. I became angry with myself and with my uncle for months. I finally came to realize that people go through hardships, and only a few remain because they refuse to quit. I turned to God to bring glory beyond my imagination. I recalled Grandpa saying, "If you fill your mouth with razors, you will spit blood." He also said, "Ashes fly back into the face of he who throws them."

I was taught by my parents to obey, but in my way of thinking I refused. They thought I was doing what they told me, but I rejected the British authority. From fifth grade to eighth grade, I refused to sing "God Bless the Queen," and when the Europeans came to the school, I refused to stand up and say, "Yes, sir." I was kicked out of school several times. Well, my dad was a British supporter, but not me.

"It is better to be loved than feared." People feared the British, but I couldn't care less.

People who get angry at a boss or someone at a higher level lose credibility. Some years ago, I worked for a boss who had dictating authority. I am a humble person, but I hate authority without respect. I did love him, but I feared him. He had no respect for others at all. Authority does not work, but caring and loving people is the best way of relating to them. They know you love them at all cost.

Here is another of Grandpa's philosophies: "A termite can do nothing to stone save lick it." If you know the truth, do not tell a lie; only the truth will stand up. This was the truth:

1. Obey the British rules, period. If you don't obey, you are not a human at all.
2. Pay your school fees from first grade to high school; if you don't pay, you are kicked out of school.
3. Sing their British anthem, which I refused to sing.

After going back to Grandpa's teaching, I started changing my way of thinking. I started reading more, and I found out that drifting people don't read or listen to audios.

Grandpa said, "The truth is like gold; keep it locked up, and you will find it exactly as you first put it away." What were the rules I found from Grandpa's teachings?

1. Be obedient.
2. Work hard.
3. Don't listen to losers.
4. Hang around with the people who are advancing in life.

"Indecision is like the stepchild—if he does not wash his hands, he is called dirty; if he does, he is wasting the water."

It's not enjoyable to grow up poor, but for anyone with a dream it is good because of all you learn. I learned in my growing up and observing both regular workers and businesspeople that "entrepreneurs focus on the maximum, and employees focus on the minimum." Entrepreneurs produce results for profits, and employees focus on the minimum because they sell their time to make money.

Focus on what you want, and don't even think about how you are going to get there. Just be willing to go after what you want, find a mentor to guide you, and be willing to do what he or she tells you.

Line Up for Your Dream Job

Kenya Railways

Some years ago in Kenya, East Africa, where I was born, I decided to go after a job that was advertised in the *East African Standard* newspaper. The opening was for a watchman for Kenya Railways. In those days, no one called you for an interview. You had to walk around looking for lineups—people in lines waiting to be picked up by an interviewer.

I found the place where they were calling for the lineup with a megaphone. People started lining up, and I joined the lineup, as well. There were many giant, tall people, and I was the skinniest young person on the line. Well, Grandpa said it this way: "A man with too much ambition cannot sleep in peace."

A person with ambition or dreams will not quit until he achieves it. You think about it all the time. Dream is powerful, but don't quit; act and forget the ups and downs.

Because I was the youngest and smallest, the man who was selecting people for interviews saw me on the line. He spotted me right away. He came right to me and said in English that I was a useless, worthless person on the lineup. He came with anger and held my neck tightly and threw me off the line. He was a European, and I was an African. I left, and all I could think of was that I still wanted to work for the Railways one day. What we think about all day and take action on, we will achieve.

My dream was to go to the Railway Training School (RTS). A friend of mine got me a job with Railways as a messenger, which I hated, but it was a stepping stone. I was an office messenger for three months, and then I applied to RTS. I was called to take tests for five days, and I passed with flying colors.

Dream big by going to see your dream at least three days a week; touch it and smell it. Repeatedly going to see your dreams three to four days a week creates action. For five years, every Friday through Sunday I walked twelve miles one way to see planes fly, and I visualized that I was flying to the United States.

Even though I was thrown out of the line, my dream was to be with Railways for at least a short time. If you were to ask me how long I would be with them, I could not tell you, but I had a dream of action and goals.

Nothing can stop you from achieving what you want in life. Within a few months of my deciding I wanted to be an employee of the East African Railways, my friend and I got together and talked about my goals and interests. He then introduced me to a man who worked for the Railways. My friend did not succeed at getting a job, but the man he introduced me to got me the job as an office messenger and then encouraged me to apply to RTS. The job was simply taking files from office to office each day. It was boring, but I had confidence that I would not be doing it for very long.

Indeed, I did not enjoy being an office messenger. I did not want my dream to decay for life. Nothing has been easy for me, but I refused to settle for a life without meaning or purpose.

Life is too short to be small and not aim high with goals and a plan of action. In six months, I was accepted at RTS, and I left the job as an office messenger on good terms. I was proud of my goal and achievement.

I think about my grandpa's philosophy, "Great events may stem from words of no importance." Listen to every conversation because you may learn great things.

"Wood touched by fire is not hard to set alight." When we have a dream or dreams, it's not hard to get actions going. When we have dreams, it's not difficult to go for what we want in spite of any opposition. My purpose was not to be an office messenger for a long time but to use this as a stepping stone.

Railway Training School

"One who runs alone cannot be outrun by another."
Stick with your dream and go to work.

I was in the seventh grade in 1959 when I got the dream of being a student at the RTS. Each year it had preliminary interviews in the summer for all the candidates who applied.

"A cow with no tail should not chase flies." If we do not have a purpose that develops passion, there is no way we can persist and not quit chasing the dream. I wanted to be one of the students at RTS so badly that I dreamed about it, and I slept on it every day. "A person with too much ambition and dreams cannot sleep in peace because he or she thinks about the dream each hour and each day."

I took tests in 1959, 1960, 1961, 1962, and 1963 to get into RTS. I failed so many times, but it did not matter to me because I knew that if I wanted to get in, I had to be different from the others who said, "I quit." Leave quitters alone and pursue your dreams.

"When a needle falls in a deep well, many people will look around the well, but only a few will go into the well to get the needle." Just follow the few with dreams, with doing, and go after your dreams with action.

Life is too short. Stay awake for it with action.

RTS was a place where people who had a dream to get a good job in their field of interest had to earn it to get into the institution. RTS was created by the East African Railways of Kenya, Uganda, and Tanzania. To get into RTS, you had to pass a preliminary exam, and if you passed it, then you had to go to the RTS campus and stay in their dorms, taking exams for five days. The competition was high because candidates came from Kenya, Uganda, Tanzania, Zanzibar Island, and surrounding countries.

In 1959, I applied to take the preliminary test to get into RTS. It was set up for only one day in a town called Machakos. I took the test, and I did not pass.

In 1960, when I was in the eighth grade, I applied again because my dream was to work for the East African Railways, and the only way to work for them was to go to RTS.

I passed the preliminary test and was invited to go to RTS to stay on campus and take tests for five days. I joined candidates from Kenya, Uganda, Tanzania, Zambia, Congo, and other countries. We stayed on campus, and they provided us with food and accommodations. On Thursday we arrived on campus, and Friday and Saturday we took the tests all day. Each day, if you did not pass the tests, they put your number on the board, and the guards walked you off through the gates. By the end of Saturday, they escorted me to the gate to go home. It meant that I had failed.

In 1961 and 1962, I applied and did not pass. Remember this: "A horse has four legs and still falls down." If you have not failed in anything, then you cannot teach, because he who learns, teaches.

"You may succeed if nobody else believes in you, but you will never succeed if you don't believe in yourself" (John C. Maxwell). Again, Grandpa said it right: "A centipede loses a leg, and it does not prevent him from walking." You can fail many times, but don't quit; stay in the game playing with a different spirit.

Note this: With a dream, go after what you want and continue taking action. Seek your mentors.

In 1963, I reapplied to RTS to see whether I could take the preliminary test. I got a letter to go for the preliminary. I went and passed it. I had only an eighth-grade education, but I never stopped reading books. Indeed, I received a letter from RTS that I needed to go to the RTS campus on a certain date to take tests for five days.

I packed and rode a bus to the RTS campus. I arrived on Thursday evening. On Friday, in the morning, they gave us instructions. We were told that there were three hundred candidates, and they were looking for thirty-three applicants who would pass the tests. Each candidate had a number, and we had to put that number on the test papers. I remember mine was number 333.

When we took the tests from Monday through Friday, each day in the afternoon, they again posted all the numbers on the board for those who did not pass. We had to look at the board to make sure our numbers weren't there. If they were on the board, we had to pack to go home. The guards escorted us out of the gate, and the gate was locked again.

The last day, Friday, they finally escorted the last group off campus. On Saturday, they instructed thirty-three candidates who passed all the exams about what date to come back to begin the training for six months.

"There is a time when we must firmly choose the course we will follow, or the endless drift of events will make the decision for us" (Herbert Prochnow).

You see, I failed the tests to get into RTS four times. I had only an eighth-grade education, and a few candidates had more education than I did. Someone said, "You will never possess what you are unwilling to pursue." Even though thirty-three candidates got into RTS, we were warned that not all of us would make it through. We graduated with only nineteen. When exams were close, I woke up at three in the morning to study. There were only three to five people studying. Set your mind to doing more than anyone else.

In 1964, I went for another training for six months to become a train conductor. They called it a guard. We were in charge of everything on the train. We had to prepare a balance sheet to show whether the train was on time or late. Every time the train stopped at a station, we had to write down the time the train arrived. We were evaluated on accuracy.

Thinking of Coming to the United States

When you have a dream, you think about it every day. Even though I was on the train almost five days a week, my mind was thinking of coming to school at Augustana Academy in South Dakota. I visualized every day coming to school, even though I knew no one in the United States. My experience is that if we do not think and visualize our dream every day, then it is not a dream but a wish.

The mind that won't quit through hard times gains a lot of experience and learns to solve problems.

From first to fourth grade we walked back and forth to school each day, eight miles one way. We had no shoes, but we had school uniforms that we had to wear. From the several villages including mine, there were between twenty and forty kids. We ate wild fruits on our walks home, if we were lucky. We learned to eat the ones that were safe.

The attitude of discouragement is too expensive—by the end of fourth grade, most of the students had quit school. Even my sister had quit. I continued going to school alone.

In fourth grade we had to walk twelve miles one way to take exams to qualify for intermediate school. For two days taking the exams, I had no food. I was hungry. After we completed the exams, I had to walk twelve miles back home. The results came out, and I was one of seventeen students passed to fifth grade.

In life, we have to make a decision to achieve whatever we want, but we have to want it so badly that we are willing to do whatever it takes. What it takes is a decision with a dream and goals and to go after it by doing. If there is no doing, then it is all nothing.

Grandpa said, "Indecision is like the stepchild. If he doesn't wash his hands, he is called dirty. If he does, he is wasting the water." If you and I are going to achieve in life, we have to decide and apply actions.

"Love is like young rice: transplanted, still it grows." I did not like school when I started first grade, but two gracious people helped me through even though they did not have any education themselves. My grandma Mary Kamene and my mom were second to none helping me by encouraging me. Let us encourage people, and those who are serious will listen and will do more because they see love and caring from you and me.

I am going to share with you my grandpa's philosophy: "When a needle falls into a deep well, many people will look into the well, but few will be ready to go down after it." Many people start something, but only a few will go after it, and the rest are wishers. This is true not only in school, business, or a profession. It is in life.

Whether in marriage, parenthood, or whatever, if we want to be financially free, we need to do what Grandpa said: "Talking with one another is loving one another." Really, I could not have succeeded in school without the encouragement of my mom and grandmother. Sometimes it was hard to go to school without food. They encouraged me all the time.

The other thing that kept me going to school was that I knew if I didn't get a good education, I would not get a good job. I had all the encouragement I needed, but the rest was up to me. To be financially free, it's up to each one of us. The dream and action.

The difference between me and other students in my village was that I was challenged spiritually and emotionally to achieve education. My dream to one day go to school in the United States started when I was in sixth grade.

Even with all the struggles I had, I kept saying that tomorrow was going to be better than yesterday. In my thinking, I did not want to say yesterday was better than today. We all face challenges, but don't surrender; don't give up. Keep pushing on.

Augustana Academy

In 1962, I was selling sewing machines in Nairobi City for Singer Sewing Company. On August 2, 1962, at ten in the morning, I was coaching Benjamin Ndonye on how to sell sewing machines. I don't know how the conversation started about coming to school in the United States. As I listened to Benjamin talk, I asked, "Do you have some addresses of colleges in the United States?" I had only an eighth-grade education, but in those days in Kenya, you could go to a technical college after eighth grade.

Ask and you will find. But if you don't ask, you will never find.

Benjamin said, "Yes. In fact, I have a friend who is going to school in the United States." Benjamin took out a little black book and wrote one address for me—Augustana Academy in Canton, South Dakota.

A dream creates a sense of urgency. The same day, I wrote to Augustana Academy. I still remember that first letter. I wrote saying that I had started working when I was very young to support my family. I asked if I could be granted a scholarship to come to the academy.

The administrator of the academy, Lowell Larson, responded to me by saying plainly, "We have no scholarship funds to give you as a foreign student at this time."

This response was, in fact, more than enough for me because I was told I had to find other ways of getting funds to come to the academy.

Grandpa said, "If the centipede loses a leg, it does not prevent him from walking."

All my life, with everything I do, I turn to God and go to work. The biggest adventure that you can take is to live the life of your dreams. The letter from the academy saying it had no funds for scholarships did not stop me from pursuing my desire to go there. I had to keep on pursuing my dream.

"Wood already touched by fire is not hard to set alight." Because heavy snow has blocked the road in front of you, it does not stop you from finding an alternate route home.

My only way was to write five letters a month to the academy asking for a scholarship so I could come to school. Remember, life is too short; we need to stay awake for it with action. Those who keep on saying one day they will get there, but take no action, are just a wind blowing, and no one knows which direction it is blowing.

Grandpa said, "No matter how full the river is, it still wants to grow."

Getting a letter saying there were no funds for a scholarship from the Augustana Academy made me want to write more letters telling them that I grew up in a family where we spelled "poor" with five O's.

I kept on writing more and more to Lowell Larson at the academy asking for a scholarship. We passed 1962 and 1963, and I had no scholarship offer. I kept on writing letters each week asking for a scholarship. If you have a dream, desire, and vision, you have to put action on it until you get it. Indeed, without action nothing will be achieved. We can talk about it day and night, but nothing will happen.

Grandpa said, "I have a cow in the sky but cannot drink her milk."

"If you are building a house and a nail breaks, do you stop building or do you change the nail?"

I kept on sending five letters a month asking for a full scholarship. I had a dream of coming to school in the United States. I ate it, slept it, and thought of it every day. I visualized it each day and at night in bed.

"Hunger is felt by a slave, and hunger is felt by a king." I was so hungry that I had to act and not just wish for my dream to come true. All the time I was sending five letters a month to the academy asking for a full scholarship, I never shared with anyone about my dream to come to the Augustana Academy. I didn't even tell my parents because I was supporting them, and telling them would have created problems for their financial support.

In 1963, I was a student being trained as a goods clerk at RTS. I received a letter from the Augustana Academy saying I had been given a partial scholarship for the fall. Remember this from Grandpa: "When a needle falls into a deep well, many people will look into the well, but few will be ready to go down after it." The partial scholarship was not enough. I received another letter from the academy telling me that if I didn't come to school in the fall, the partial scholarship would be taken away. I refused to surrender my dreams. I kept on sending more letters a month, more than five, asking for a full scholarship. Can you imagine what the administrator was thinking receiving more than five letters a month with a polite request for a full scholarship?

"Unless you call out, who will open the door?"

Persist until you get it. Finally, the board of directors found that I was not going to give up. The board of directors through administrator Larson wrote a letter telling me that there was a lady not far from Augustana Academy named Mabel Broadland. She had offered to cover the rest of the scholarship. I was offered a partial scholarship by the academy, and Mabel Broadland would pay for the other portion.

I also received a letter from the academy saying that if I didn't come to school that fall, they would take this scholarship away from me. "Wood already touched by fire is not hard to set alight."

I had an incessant dream to come to school in the United States. When you have a dream, you sleep on it and think of it every minute. I slept it, I ate it, and every day I envisioned coming to school at the academy. I could not imagine losing the scholarship. All I could do was fight for it by sending ten letters a month to the academy. I told them that I was a teenager and that I had started working when I was in first grade. I looked after livestock for an uncle, and I had no money for the airfare to fly to school in the fall. In those days, the American embassy also required a student to have at least $3,000, which it called "pocket funds," to come into the United States. I had no funds for airfare or pocket money. "He who cannot dance will say the drum is bad."

I grew with faith in God and prayer each day, three and four times a day. I prayed privately to God, and all I requested was to obey and follow Him in my lifetime.

During this time, some people found out I was planning to come to school in the United States with only an eighth-grade education. I had so many people telling me day and night I was not smart enough, and my parents had nothing. I could not go to the United States with only an eighth-grade education.

In fact, when I came to high school at the Augustana Academy, not many people came to school with only an eighth-grade education.

"An intelligent enemy is better than a stupid friend."

All the people told me that I could not make it to the United States because my parents were poor and never went to school to know how to read and write. Yes, I agree that in my dad's family we were so poor that we spelled "poor" with five O's. Poor is when you go to bed for four days without food. Pay no attention to those who want to go between home and work for forty-five to sixty-five years. Life is too short; pay attention to it with actions. When you have a dream, you focus on your own business.

"Living is worthless without a dream."

I was supposed to come to school in the fall of 1964, and I did not make it because I had no money for airfare. "By trying often the monkey learns to jump from the tree."

Because I could not make it in the fall of 1964, I kept on sending more letters to the administrator at Augustana Academy. I repeated the story that I had no money for transportation. I tried to come by ship and work on the ship, but it was going to take too long to get to the United States and to the Augustana Academy.

During this time, I was getting letters from the academy saying that if I did not make it in the fall, they would take the scholarship away from me. They kept telling me they had many students who wanted to come to school.

"Unless you call out, who will open the door?"

When you want something badly enough, you will find a way to get it by going after it.

I looked at the Augustana Academy catalogue they had sent me. I went through all the names of the board of directors, looking at the names and professions. I found Pastor Alvin Petersen's name. The same day, I wrote to him asking for financial help so that I could fly to the United States to attend Augustana Academy. Pastor Petersen replied to my letter, saying that he had communicated with the registrar at the academy, and he could not be assured that I was accepted there.

"Let your love be like the misty rain, coming softly but flooding the river."

I wanted to come to school in the United States so badly, and I was willing to do whatever it took. I knew that nothing comes easy in life. Anything we achieve easily does not last long, but the things we want to last we have to work for. I always turned to prayer any time I had challenges.

Pastor Petersen wrote to me on October 19, 1966, asking me, "How did you happen to contact me? I am a pastor of the Lutheran Student Foundation, Inc., at the University of Nebraska, and some students are interested in finding out more about you. Would you be able to give me some references from persons who know you to whom I might write about you wanting to come to this country and the possibility of your being able to do high school studies?"

"The opportunity that God sends to you or me does not wake up who is asleep."

Being in the United States

"A person who does not travel says his mother cooks the best food" (Grandpa Tumbo).

When I was in Kenya, I thought we had the best food—until I got to the United States and found they had the best food. I love traveling so much.

During my time in Kenya, I heard so many stories about the struggles people went through coming to this country, like walking six hundred miles to get a passport or visa. Just as it still is today, people committed to losing their lives in order to come to the United States. Some die on the sea, and those who make it to this country have incessant dreams to own their own business. These people do all kinds of odd jobs that don't pay much, but they have long-term goals.

I had never heard of the Internet marketing business, in which I am involved now, until my friend and mentor, Dan, showed it to me. I did not know him much at all. He and I met at my friend's birthday party.

I was busy working sixty hours a week and going to law school thirty hours a week. My wife, Sandy, was working as a registered nurse and going to school for her master's degree in nursing. We had a four-year-old and a two-year-old. Did we have any time? Many people would have said, "No, I do not have time for something like this." Yes, we had no time, but I knew unless you call out, who will open the door? We did not try to figure out why Internet marketing development could not work; we had dreams, and we were coachable.

Dr. Robert Anthony said it right: "Forget about all the reasons why something may not work. You only need one good reason why it will."

Some years ago, when I was a freshman at Augustana College, I wrote this: "You are playing with American financial freedom, which makes so many struggle and die in the ocean and on dry land coming to this country. Many leave their parents, brothers, sisters, wives and husbands, friends, and many other things to come for financial freedom and are willing to work for it."

If anyone can tolerate where they are now financially, or maybe they have marriage challenges, then they are not willing to change. Indeed, there is no cure that does not cost.

I have enjoyed the United States, and I continue touching the people who act on their incessant dreams.

Zig Ziglar for many years said, "If you are willing to help many people to get what they want, you will never worry about yourself financially." Grandpa said it right: "It is a bad child who does not take advice."

I came to this country with forty-five dollars, not knowing anyone. Today I have several mentors who helped me grow, such as Jerry Meadows, Bert Gulick, and Dan Smith. I am so blessed. Money, people, opportunity, and time are excuses. These people have the dreams, and it does not matter what size. Papa Tumbo said, "I have a cow in the sky but cannot drink her milk." Very precisely he meant, "I have a dream, but I don't want to work hard to achieve it."

Papa Tumbo had two hundred grandkids, and in the evenings we made a fire close to the door of the place where the cows rested in the evening. Papa Tumbo told stories to the grandkids, and all the dads were there. They all listened to the stories and proverbs. Among the two hundred grandkids, I wrote down everything he said. Note this very well: everyone in my village counted me as a failure. I was a loner and a thinker. Papa Tumbo said this proverb, and I woke up as I wrote it down: "Talking with another is loving one another."

Papa Tumbo also said this one evening: "Do not dispose of the monkey's tail before he is dead." I asked our gracious papa what it meant. He smiled courageously and said, "Never give up on anyone unless he or she gives up on himself or herself."

Our parents were our first home, and without them we would have been nothing. They did everything to make sure that we grew with discipline and respect for the elders and other people. They taught us work ethic and to not quit until the job was done. They indeed taught us by example to rise up above our circumstances.

Both Mom and Dad had no education but had common sense. They believed in working for themselves by raising livestock such as cattle, goats, sheep, and chickens. They had four farms in different areas. These farms were four to ten miles away. We had oxen to pull the plow to these farms. We plowed from seven in the morning to seven in the evening without any food.

Our parents served Nzaini village and the surroundings. They enjoyed being with other people and talking with them. Grandpa used to say that talking to one another was having the food of the soul and learning from one another.

When the world gets in my face, I say "Have a nice day" with a smile. Grandpa used to say, "A fool looks for dung where the cow has never been browsed." This proverb tells it fully and clearly. If the dream has no melody, nothing will happen.

There is great power in focusing on what you want. It seems like such an obvious statement, yet most of us miss it. Dreams can come true. You can get to a place called extraordinary in what you choose to do. Yes, you can find love deeper than you have ever imagined. But you need a dream and a focus. My parents had no education but made a difference in others' lives. They had all of the above—the dream and the focus.

The person who tries to do everything accomplishes nothing. This is what most people try to do. Our parents took one thing at a time and focused on it.

Really, what you focus on grows. What you concentrate on is what you see more of in your life. Focus on financial mastery, and you will see your economic life improve.

Mom and Dad focused on us, seven children by the time my younger siblings were born, but they had so many challenges, such as going without food for four days. They kept saying they would find food for us. Finally, after four days they found food—one glass of milk that all of us shared. Dream big and ignore the facts, because facts don't last that long.

Nicholas Isika

I remember my parents looking for food and water during the drought. When they found it, they had to walk twelve miles to get the water to drink, wash clothes in the river with dirty water, and many other things that happened.

I have found that the bigger the dream, the more obstacles I face. My mission is straightforward: I want to help human beings who have dreams to become financially free and turn to the power of God so they can do whatever they want to do. I hear people say money is not everything, but lack of money will buy plenty of unhappiness. I have a passion to do my part to make this world a better place. I am an Internet entrepreneur and visionary. I specialize in helping entrepreneurs create financial freedom from the inside out. It is not just a business to me; it is a calling. Yes, when we have a big want in the face of adversity, we will be tested along the way.

Mom and Dad were tested through their struggles, and that is why I am in the United States today—because I learned from them not to give up. We have to know that life tests the big dreamers; the people with passion change the world.

I came into this world with nothing, and I am going to leave it with nothing but accomplishments. I want you to think about the truth I shared with you about Mom and Dad. They served the villagers by feeding the kids in the village when they had food. They shared me with the villagers to look after their livestock, take care of the elders, and do many other things. Reflect on what you want to stand for and what your impact will be. Indeed, contemplate the words of Dr. Garth Taylor: "Until I have no breath to breathe, I will continue to do this because I think I was chosen for this, not for money, not for compensation, but just to make the quality of life of fellow human beings better."

Dream Work

In 1962, I started to work for Singer Sewing Company as a salesman. I did not want to be a salesman, but I had to do something to earn money. I did not have many options with only an eighth-grade education.

We sold door-to-door by asking people if they liked to sew clothes. We knocked on so many doors, but 95 percent were nos and only 5 percent were yeses.

I came up with an idea to sell more sewing machines, and we began leaving machines for people to use for two days. Our sales increased by 10 percent. We had only two vans to deliver machines. As sales increased, they bought two more vans to deliver machines to people for trials. In six months, I was promoted to sales manager. As a sales manager, I was paid a salary and a commission on the amount of sales my team generated each month. I got tired of walking door-to-door, so I bought a bicycle. It had no gears at all.

We worked from eight in the morning to nine at night Monday through Friday knocking on doors. The more people we served by selling sewing machines, the more commission we received. The sales representatives who did not knock on a lot of doors did not earn a lot of money. We had to make it fun and exciting. Was it easy? No, but we had to put in the time and effort.

When I was promoted to sales manager, I could ask a driver to take me to see customers. I usually chose to ride my bike, but once in a while, if I had customers more than sixty miles away, I had to ask the driver to take me there.

With the driver, I took six sewing machines and dropped them to prospects to try. It was a product sample. Some people said no before I built a relationship with them, but then down the road they bought sewing machines. Sometimes when I went to the country to visit my parents, I brought gifts to some of my customers and to the nos with whom I built relationships. I brought corn, beans, sugar, or something small.

The more people we serve, the more joy, energy, and belief we create within us and the more rewards we get. I used to visit some of my customers in the hospital if they were sick.

Someone made this profound statement: "When you serve the class, you will live with the masses, but when you serve the masses, you will live with the class."

Indeed, life is serving others, and the more we serve, the happier and more energetic we become.

When you see an opportunity, don't underestimate it by asking others who have accomplished nothing. When a stranger in the streets of Nairobi City approached me about coming to work for Singer Sewing Company, I had no clue it would lead me to meet Benjamin, who gave me the address of Augustana Academy. Little did I know it would lead to an everlasting memory.

In reality, Singer Sewing Company made a lot of money for itself and paid me as little as it could. This happens to people in the world; they get a job and get stuck. In most jobs, the rewards are like what Grandpa used to say: "Having a job is almost like milking a cow with no milk."

"Good millet is known at the harvest."

I had a purpose, and I was willing to pursue it at all costs. If you have a purpose and you are willing to pursue it, to achieve it, you will face challenges as I did.

This is where it all started with a conversation on August 2, 1962, and correspondence with Augustana Academy. Great events may stem from words of no importance.

Wanting Something Badly Enough Brings No Surrender

"Fine words do not produce food."

In life, we find people who are excited about achieving their dreams, are presented with challenges, and then quit. I had no money to come to school in the United States, and one of my classmates was also trying to come to school in Rapid City. My friend had a full scholarship except airfare. Because we had the same purpose, I decided to ask him if there were any organizations in the area that could help students who wanted to go to school in the United States. My friend gave me the address of a person who was well known in our area and who raised a lot of funds for students who were going overseas for further education.

If you have a dream, act. I had no money to do anything, so I borrowed money from a person I did not know very well. I have no idea, even today, why this stranger loaned me money. It was Friday. I rode on a bus for 163 miles to talk to this man who raised funds for students going overseas for higher education. On that Friday at three in the afternoon, I got to his office. I met the gentleman and introduced myself. We were from the same tribe, Kamba tribe. He was a very gracious man. I told him that I was *destined* to go to school in the United States at the Augustana Academy, but I had no funds for airfare. Mind you, when I went to see this gentleman, all I needed was airfare.

Grandpa Mbinda, my mom's father, said it this way: "As the wound inflames the finger, so thought inflames the mind." The man I went to see was so pleasant to me. I told him about myself, and I told him that I had an eighth-grade education.

A Guinea proverb says, "He who has done evil, expects evil." This man told me to my face that in two weeks he would be raising funds for two other students, and I was a third one. His comment then was that we would now be raising funds for an eighth-grader going for further education in the United States, but I had no clue what he meant. It sounded like it was a joke because I didn't have a high school education like the other two guys.

Get this. He told me they had no place to meet and raise funds in Nairobi City. I told him that I could find a place at the East African Railways at the main hall. Yes, I booked the fundraising on the date he told me. On Saturday the gentleman came, and I introduced him to the people. The hall was packed to maximum. He spoke very well and mentioned the three people for whom he was raising the funds. One comment he made disappointed me. He told the crowd that there was a young lad with only an eighth-grade education trying to go to school in the United States. He said right there in front of me, "If you want to go for further education, you need to have a high school education." I knew he was talking about me.

Grandpa Tumbo said it well: "What has blown away cannot be found again." Here is the story about raising funds on that Saturday. Salute it and appreciate it with your full heart.

Indeed, on that Saturday I booked the hall and paid for it, and he raised a lot of funds that day. Here is an amazing bit of education for you and me. The other two students who were going for further education in the United States got funds that day, and I got *nothing*. The gentleman who was conducting the fundraising told me I would get funds the next time. That was the end of that; I never heard from him again. And the two guys who received the funding never made it to school in the United States at all.

My question is, why do some people see an opportunity and act on it, and others reject it? It is a mystery to me, but the dream is the only answer.

Howard Schultz, founder of Starbucks, said, "I believe life is a series of near misses. A lot of what we ascribe to luck is not luck at all. It is seizing the day and accepting responsibility for your future. It is seeing what other people don't see and pursuing that vision."

Some years ago, I visited Kenya. I left the United States for Kenya without a valid passport. I had tried to renew my passport with the Kenyan embassy in New York. They told me it would take a month to get it renewed, so I left for Kenya with my old passport. I then had a tough time renewing my passport. One day I happened to meet a friend of mine in the streets of Nairobi City. We talked for a few minutes, and I told him that I had come without a valid passport. He asked if I had my invalid passport with me. I said yes. My friend said, "Let's go to the immigration office." We walked upstairs to the chief officer in the immigration office. My friend introduced me and explained my situation to him, and within half an hour I had a valid passport.

Here is the point I am making. When my friend and I were just about half a mile from the immigration office, I heard someone shouting my name. I turned around, and it was my friend Raphel, who was trying to come to school in Cedar Rapids, Iowa. He was one of the guys given funds during the fundraising where I did not get anything at all. As Raphel and I talked, he said, "You were lucky that you made it to school in the United States." I asked him what had happened to him. He said, "I had everything set up to fly to the United States to school, but I was discouraged by my friends not to waste my time going to school." Raphel added that his friends told him that American academics were hard because you had to go to school and also work. I told Raphel that that was what I was doing and it did not bother me at all. Raphel added, "I still wish I could go to school in the United States, but I am too old." I told him that Grandpa used to say, "You are old when you are dead."

Thomas Edison said, "Opportunity is missed by most people because it is dressed in overalls and looks like work."

Courage to Come to the United States

Grandpa said, "Indecision is like the stepchild. If he doesn't wash his hands, he is called dirty; if he does, he is wasting the water."

I made the decision to come to school at Augustana Academy when no one without a high school education was permitted by the immigration department to come to school in the United States.

After five years of courage and disappointment, I got airfare from Pastor Alvin Petersen on February 4, 1967. Pastor Petersen sent the money to my former teacher in seventh grade, Peter Makau. That same day, I rode a bus 163 miles to see my parents and tell them I was flying to the United States the next day to go to school. This was a surprise to my parents. My dad asked me where I got the money for my airfare. His thoughts were that I was working as a train conductor for East African Railways, and he asked me if I had stolen the money from the railways. I told my loving, gracious dad, "God provided me with the money." Both Dad and Mom knew my faith in God was very strong. God has given me visions or feelings. My wife, Sandy, can say more about this, because she used to think I was crazy when I told her the things God showed me and what would happen.

When I told Dad I would be flying to the United States at three forty-five in the afternoon on February 5, 1967, he talked to the villagers from Nzaini and hired two buses to come see me take off.

Grandpa said, "When a mouse laughs at a cat, there is a hole nearby." These are the people who don't have dreams. So many of my friends had laughed at me because my parents were so poor that they spelled *poor* with five *o*'s. Never think about people telling you that you cannot do what you decide to do. I had other friends who encouraged me. John Makau is a man of love and encouragement. He took care of me when I was nothing. Pastor Samuel K. Kikelo, Wallace Waithaka, and John Makau—these people are special to me, even today.

Grandpa Mbinda said, "There is no one who became rich because he broke a holiday, and no one who became fat because he broke a fast."

I had never flown on an airplane before. On February 5, 1967, I said good-bye, shaking hands with more than sixty people from Nzaini. My gracious dad had created a sense of urgency in the village to come to Nairobi Airport to see me take off. That day, I mailed my resignation to East African Railways from Nairobi Airport. Just imagine what was going through my mind after five years of struggle.

At three in the afternoon, they announced that Pan Am flight 151 would be leaving at three forty-five.

In my mind, I was thinking I was going to the Nairobi Airport to see planes flying as I had every Friday, Saturday, and Sunday when I would visualize my dream of flying to school in the United States.

Dream and Be Obsessed

From Nairobi to Manhattan

Every day when I was a train conductor traveling to Kampala, Uganda, Dar es Salaam, Tanzania, and Kenya, I was thinking about going to school in the United States. I communicated with God all the time. When you are really hungry, you think of your dream each hour, each day. If we don't think of our dream each day, we won't work for it or fight for it at all.

The flight took off from Nairobi to Kampala, Uganda; Ghana; Nigeria; Monrovia; and Liberia, and the last stop was Senegal.

Pan Am had super service. We flew all night. Flying over the ocean through the night, my heart was saying, "Spend much time in secret with Jesus alone."

The pilot started announcing that we were close to New York City, and we would be landing at JFK airport. Mind you, I had never been on an airplane before. We started going around and around in the air at JFK, and the pilot said they were clearing a runway for the plane to land. As the plane was flying around and around, I saw some white insects in the air. I turned to the gentleman sitting next to me and said, "Look at those white insects flying around."

This gentleman looked at me and replied, "Sir, those are not white insects."

I asked him, "What are they?"

His response was, "You will know when you get off the plane."

Some people think that to be strong is to never feel pain. In reality, the strongest people are the ones who feel it, understand it, and accept it.

In those days, when you got off the plane, you had to walk from the field to the airport. As people were getting out of the plane at JFK, they started putting on coats, boots, and hats, and I was just in a plain black suit with none of what they were putting on to keep warm. You can imagine, at seventeen degrees below zero, people were looking at me. These people must have been thinking that I was wearing two or three pairs of long johns, and I did not even know what they were back then.

As I went through Immigration, an officer wearing a black uniform asked me to show him my visa and passport. He looked at them and asked me if I was going to South Dakota. I said yes. His comment was, "What are you going to do in South Dakota? All they have is American Indians."

As Grandpa said, "Don't ask what is being born; you are going to see the child." So I did not ask the officer another question. I was so excited to see Indians because in Kenya I associated with Indians from India.

I got done with Immigration, and I was free and at peace in my mind.

I had a letter from my friend Peter Makau in my hand with directions to where he lived in Manhattan. Peter was my math teacher in seventh grade in Kenya before he came for further education in the United States. He and I were great friends. He liked me because I was obedient and a good student.

I went outside to wait for a bus to take me to Manhattan. Well, I did not know New York City, and many people were going in every direction, all wearing winter clothes. I had never seen so many people in my life. To me, it looked like a zoo full of people. I was standing outside waiting for the bus in a plain suit at a temperature of seventeen degrees below zero. That is what I call "ignorance has no defense." I was afraid of talking to anyone because I thought they might get my forty-five dollars, the only money I had.

Note this. Whatever makes you feel bad, leave it. Whatever makes you smile, keep it. After standing outside for forty-five minutes at JFK waiting for a bus, I decided to find someone I could talk to for directions to Manhattan.

"The man who can drive himself further once the effort gets painful is the man who will win" (Roger Bannister).

I prayed at seventeen degrees below zero, "God is the source of comfort and hope for me now." I have always depended on God's direction, but I go after what I want. It has been that way all my life.

Standing outside at JFK, I did not know where I was going even though I had a letter with directions from Professor Makau. I had never been in a foreign country, but here I was standing outside in weather of seventeen degrees below zero wearing a black suit without overshoes or a winter coat. I was freezing so badly that I stopped having pain.

Here is what happens: you get the courage to do anything. As afraid as I was, I saw a man passing by. He was tall and wearing a brown leather coat with a hood covering his head against the cold. I said, "Excuse me, sir."

He responded, "Yes, sir."

I asked this gentleman, "How do I get to this place?" I gave him the letter I had from Professor Makau.

He read it, and his question was, "How long have you been in the United States?"

I said, "Forty-five minutes."

He said, "Poor boy."

This gentleman introduced himself. He said his name was Joe Samuelson from Chicago, Illinois, and added that he was a businessman. As he spoke, smoke came from his mouth. I was about to run, but I asked, "Why do you have smoke coming from your mouth?"

He said, "It is seventeen degrees below zero, and it is very cold. When it is cold, we breathe cold air, and when we breathe it out it looks like smoke."

He told me, "Manhattan is about fifteen miles from here, but I will take you there." I tried to pick up my suitcase, which had only one suit, two changes of underwear, and my documents. I could not even bend my fingers. They were frozen. So Mr. Samuelson said he would pick it up. He did, and then he gave these instructions. He told me that from here at JFK, we would ride a bus to the subway and that I should not pay for anything at all. He added, "I will take care of everything."

We got on a bus, and I just followed Mr. Samuelson's instructions. We got off the bus, and then he said to me, "Now we are catching a subway." You can imagine what I was thinking all the way: *This gentleman, Joe Samuelson, will take me someplace and get my forty-five dollars.* Then I recalled what Grandpa Tumbo said: "Do not call the forest that shelters you a jungle."

I had been a train conductor in Kenya, but I had never seen anything like a subway. Mr. Samuelson and I got on the subway train. It was so noisy I could not hear Mr. Samuelson talking to me.

We got off the train and walked a few blocks to Professor Makau's place on the thirteenth floor. Mr. Samuelson knocked on the door, and Professor Makau opened it. They introduced themselves to each other. Mr. Samuelson asked Professor Makau, "Why did you not tell this gentleman that we have bad weather during this time?" Professor Makau said he had forgotten.

Mr. Samuelson, who had a very successful business, offered to help a young lad who knew nothing about the United States. He was a gracious man to help me all the way. Mr. Samuelson and I communicated for five years after this loving event. He is more than a businessman, but a man of serving.

Here is something I have learned from the people in my life. Nelson Mandela was put in jail for twenty-seven years in South Africa, but he told those who put him in jail, "Come and let us work together." Mother Teresa did not know anything about computers or the Internet and did not have a lot of education. And yet when she was called, both famous and ordinary people came to say good-bye to her. The attendance at her funeral showed that she had a loving heart. Professor Makau was like that to everyone he met or taught.

I stayed with Professor Makau for four days. I had a sense of urgency to get to Augustana Academy in South Dakota to fulfill my dream.

On A Greyhound Bus

On February 10, 1967, Professor Makau took me to the Greyhound bus at two in the afternoon to ride to South Dakota. As I rode the bus, every two hours I asked the driver, "Are we close to Sioux Falls, South Dakota, yet?" I was sitting behind the driver. After a while, it came time for the drivers to exchange driving. Before the first driver left the bus, he told the second driver to help me and not be upset with me. Have a big heart, but have a dream to accomplish your goals.

My grandpa Tumbo said, "Those who don't travel say their mother cooks the best food." Mind you, I came from a different culture, and when we went to any restaurant we knew what we wanted to order. Every place the Greyhound bus stopped, we had to go to a restaurant to eat. It was interesting to me that every time we went to a restaurant, they gave me this book that had food pictures in it. Then they came back and asked me what I wanted to order. I had learned about hamburgers when I was in New York with Professor Makau, so whenever I was asked what I wanted to order, I told them coffee and a hamburger. Never be ashamed of anything you do if it is part of your dream.

On February 11, 1967, we got to Sioux Falls, South Dakota, at nine thirty at night. I thought I was in Canton, South Dakota, home to Augustana Academy.

Indeed, those who do not travel think they are smarter than the average bear. At ten o'clock, the Sioux Falls bus depot started closing, and they told me, "Sir, we are closing now." I asked them if this was Canton, South Dakota, and they said politely, "No, sir. This is Sioux Falls."

I asked them how far from here to Canton, and they said thirty miles. I did not care about the cost because I had the dream to get to Canton, South Dakota, to go to school at the academy. So I got a cab, and the driver asked me if I knew how many miles it was from Sioux Falls to Canton. He said it was thirty miles. My words to him were that I did not care. Here is the point I want to make precisely to you—when we have a dream to accomplish anything in life, there are no ifs or buts. We must do what we have to in spite of disappointments.

The cab driver told me he would speed for me, which he did. When we got to the academy at about ten thirty, the acting president, Luther Simpson, paid the driver six dollars.

If we want to accomplish anything, it is not only a positive attitude but a dream that needs to be in our hearts every day. If there is no dream, there is no hope. And where there is no hope, there is nothing.

Let me go back to my arrival at the Sioux Falls bus station. I called Luther Simpson and asked him to come pick me up in downtown Canton. So he sent his daughter with one the teacher, who became my typing teacher at Augustana Academy, to pick me up. He was quite surprised when she called and told him she could not find Nicholas Isika.

The following Monday I started high school. I got together with the principal, Mr. Boyum. He told me, "We want to test you by picking all the subjects and classes for you this year." Mr. Boyum, who had a deep and commanding voice, said, "If you do well this year in the classes I select for you, then we will think of more." I did not know what he meant. This is what I have learned in my life's adventures—if I have to accomplish anything in life for which I do not have a passion, having a "must" is the key, not a "should" or anything else.

After I was at the academy for two years, Mr. Boyum called me into his office and told me that I would be graduating that year and going on to Augustana College.

My question was, "Do you think I can handle college studies?"

He said, "Nicholas, you proved in two years that you can do college work in all the subjects we assigned you to." Again, courage and rivers of doubt came back to me. I applied to Columbia University in New York but did not receive a scholarship.

I went to Augustana College and completed my studies with a full scholarship for four years. Without the scholarship, I would not have made it through. I owe the college a big debt.

I always had courage to accomplish any dream, even though I was afraid. No matter what, I had in my heart the dream to do it.

Let's take inventory about me. Indeed, I am not saying that I am better than anyone else. Here is my opinion: It is not passion, not intelligence, not luck, and not where we come from that matters. Action is the only thing that will lead us to our dreams or purpose. When we have action for our dream, not a "should" but a "must," we will do whatever it takes.

"The man who can drive himself further once the effort gets painful is the man who will win" (Roger Bannister).

Grandpa Tumbo said, "By trying often, the monkey learns to jump from the tree."

Here are more of Grandpa's proverbs.

"Confiding a secret of success to an unworthy person is like carrying grain in a bag with a hole."

"Because he has no eyes, he says that eyes smell bad." This is someone who has no dreams. Life is full of challenges and the excitement of whom we associate with. Whomever we associate with, we become like them. Grandpa Tumbo said, "No one lives with someone with smallpox and fails to get smallpox." If we hang around with people who don't read and who have no dreams, we become like them.

Who Am I?

At the age of ten, I started asking myself, *who am I?* I started defining who I was. I defined that I love my God, I am ambitious, and I must do what I decide to do. I am a loving person, and I don't prejudge other people.

Our lives are defined by our beliefs and convictions, and our spirit determines how we are going to live. I had fear as a teenager struggling to come to school in the United States. I had discouragements, but courage kept me going. On February 5, 1967, at three forty-five, when I boarded Pan Am flight 151, all I could think about was how I had worked hard to make it to school in the United States, and I prayed to God all the time.

The *East African Standard* newspaper ran a story about people who hear the call and respond and people who hear the call and act as if they did not hear it. Here is the story:

> Once a hyena was walking in the dark at night, and he talked to the rock, but the rock did not respond. The hyena talked again to the rock, and the rock did not respond. Finally, the hyena told the rock, "Even if you don't respond, you heard me."

So define who you are, find your action, and go for it, but find mentors who will pick you up when you fall. Raise your standard and demand more from yourself. Standards turn you from should to must. We create results when we raise our standards.

I grew up in a loving home. Mom and Dad were a team raising us kids. My two sisters and I had to do everything that had to be done. My sisters had to cook every time we had food in the house. The food we had to eat every day, if we had it, was beans and white corn. My sisters washed our clothes in the river where there were rocks because you had to hit the clothes on the rocks to get them clean. All three of us had to milk the cows in the morning and in the evening. Most of the time, I looked after the livestock for our family and the neighbors in the village.

Yes, food was rare during the drought. It looked like every two years we had a drought. During the rainy season, people harvested a lot of food, such as beans, corn, cassava, millet, wheat, and potatoes. Really, we did not have a lot of vegetables because of the drought.

In Kenya, we can have either a long rainy season, which lasts three to four months, or a short rainy season, which lasts two months. People knew that if we did not get a long rainy season, drought was coming.

Mind you, not everyone in the village had big farms like my parents'.

The tradition was that the elder son always inherited bigger land, and the land was given by the father. Girls did not inherit anything at all. Women were for dowry. It was a tradition and a strong one.

During the drought, people who had extra food shared it with the other villagers and relatives. Mom had so much compassion for people, she shared our food with the villagers and with her three brothers and two sisters. Her brothers and sisters had family. I remember them coming to our home every week to get some food. When there was a famine because of drought, and food was shared, the food did not last long. That is why we went for four or more days without food. We were taught that family affairs are not for the public to know. We acted all the time as if we had eaten. Mom and Dad taught us to be hard workers and not quit anything we start. In my Kamba tribe, quitting is considered cowardly. A coward cannot lead people or achieve anything in life. A coward cannot be financially free because his financial freedom is determined by how many hours he works per day and for a week and for a month.

Men as well off as my dad had to plow the farms before the rain fell, using oxen to pull the plows. Our farms were four miles to ten miles away from the village. I did the plowing with my dad because my three brothers were not yet born. We plowed all day without eating any food. Sometimes when we got home there was no food, and we had to eat bananas.

My dad lived a quiet and peaceful life. In all my life, I never saw my dad get angry even though he was offended at times by our relatives. For example, one of his relatives took a banana farm owned by my dad, but I never saw Dad angry at him. Dad and Mom lived a life of giving and serving others. When other men were on their second or third wife, Dad and Mom remained together and took care of us. Grandpa always said, "Marriage is more than four legs in a bed." He said the same thing about love. My parents focused on raising good children, and they did. They focused on farming to feed the family and sharing food and many other things. They allowed other people to use their oxen to plow their farms.

In life, we focus on what we *want*. Mom, Dad and grandmothers Mary Kamene and Miriam Munyiva focused on loving me and encouraging me to do my best. From time to time, they told me to be me and focus on what I want. Encouragement is good. I am in the United States because they believed in me.

Free Enterprise

One day, Grandpa Mbinda, on my mom's side, was going to sell tobacco in the market fifteen miles away. Grandpa asked me if I could ride my bike ahead of him. I said, "Yes, Grandpa." I was in third grade. School was out, and I was living with him and Grandma. I can say that I was blessed with loving grandparents. I spent a lot of time with them rather than spending time with kids my age.

I got to the market before Grandpa, and I waited there for him to arrive. Finally, Grandpa got to the market at about two in the afternoon, and I helped him set up his tobacco-selling place. With respect for Grandpa, I asked him whether I could go around riding my bike. This bike had no gears, and it was all manual. I bought it with my own money. I rode my bike around and around in the market. Mind you, many women were selling bananas in the market. Well, no one can predict what will happen when you are driving, flying, or operating equipment.

By accident, I ran over a woman's bananas with my bike. I smashed a lot of them. The woman took my bike and told me that if I didn't come up with the money to pay for her smashed bananas, she would take my bike and sell it. Remember, I was brought up with respect for people.

Grandpa Mbinda was a man of his word, and he provided for his family well. I was scared to tell Grandpa what had happened. Grandpa said nothing except, "Come with me and show me the woman and the bike." I took Grandpa to the woman. She was shouting, but Grandpa asked her how much the bananas cost that his grandson Mutiso had run over. I listened and prayed. Well, Grandpa and the lady agreed on the amount Grandpa had to pay. Grandpa paid it, and I got my bike. I always tell people, never go anyplace without money, because you may run over someone else's bananas as I did. Money is good, not evil. Without money, you will buy plenty of unhappiness. Money is a tool. The more money we have, the more choices we have to do whatever it is we want to do.

Shining as Parents and Grandparents

As I was growing up, I don't remember ever missing my parents or grandparents. When we came home from school, they were at home. Any time, they were always there. They taught us how to work hard and not worry about past events—good or bad. Their emphasis was that the past had been written with disappearing ink, and there was nothing you could do about it. So many of the things our parents and grandparents taught us were about climbing tall trees, jumping in rivers, or killing snakes. They were about living in the present and learning to respond with courage to what life gave us. I was afraid of heights, and I do not have that fear anymore.

Try not to teach your fears to your children. Introduce them instead to what is possible.

Our parents led by example. The best way they influenced us was by doing what they preached, not just talking about it.

They inspired us. They gave us huge ideas about how to view the world. They talked about how we would travel, eat different kinds of food, meet different people, and so many other things.

I remember one statement my mom made when I passed the exam for fifth grade. I came home tired and wondering whether I had passed. I told my mom I didn't know how I had done on the exams. Her response was, "Don't look back unless it's a good view." Mom was right. I decided not to look back because the view was not always good.

Our parents and grandparents were devoted to us children. We were the number-one priority for them. They entertained us by telling stories and African proverbs like:

"Being well dressed will not prevent one from being poor."

"He who does not mend his clothes will soon have none."

"A silly daughter teaches her mother how to bear children."

"Mutual affection gives each his share."

"Knowledge is like a garden; if it is not cultivated, it cannot be harvested."

"If there were no elephants in the jungle, the buffalo would be a great animal."

In those days, Africans liked to tell proverbs because proverbs were the daughters of experience. They were the horses of conversation. When a conversation lags, a proverb will revive it.

This is why "a wise man who knows proverbs reconciles difficulties."

These proverbs taught us to grow from the inside out because, when you hear them, there is no other teacher but your own soul.

Grandmothers are special with understanding hearts. When others lose their faith in you, that is just when theirs will start.

What was special about both my grandmothers, Miriam Munyiva and Mary Kamene, was that they were strong in their faith in God, in love, and in their encouragements for me all the time.

Miriam was my grandmother on my mother's side, and Mary was on my father's side. Miriam and Mary were destined in faith. They were strong Christians and loving people. They believed in Matthew 5:8, "Blessed are the pure in heart, for they shall see God." Both of them encouraged me to accomplish things. They encouraged all the grandchildren, but evidently the others did not want to listen and practice all the time. I was in many ways victimized by the other grandkids, but I knew they did not have wisdom like my grandmothers. Most of the time, I hung around my grandparents to learn faith in God and to grasp the wisdom they had.

I learned by watching my parents and grandparents and by listening to their coaching. Grandma Miriam used to preach on the other side of the mountains every Saturday from six to seven thirty in the morning. She used an African megaphone and preached that "salvation is created in the midst of the earth, oh God ..."

I learned that human beings move when their emotions are moved. Our grandparents and parents taught us to smile when we met people. It was so important to smile even during any life challenges. I still respect this teaching today.

An unknown person said, "A smile is electricity, and life is the battery. Whenever you smile, the battery gets charged, and a beautiful day is activated." Smile, please.

My special Grandma Miriam asked me if I could join her in preaching on the mountains, and I did. I had my own megaphone, and both of us preached every Saturday.

Of course, when you make any good commitment, you will find people of your age and older going against it. I had some shouts from boys my age telling me I was missing the fun in life. Yes, I was told I was naïve to follow the old people. My response was that I had a commitment to God and my grandma.

Here is what I learned from my grandparents: "When a Masai or Moran warrior does not want to dance, he says the Earth has bumps." Indeed, when you find this blaming discouragement in yourself and find yourself spreading negatives to something you don't want to do, the truth is you tried and failed because you did not work at it. You listened instead to the people who have no courage to achieve. They talk about doing what they say they will do, but they actually do nothing.

You will find discouragements from other people in church, business, or anything else you want to do. Grandpa said, "If a dead tree falls, it carries with it a live one."

Grandpa Mbinda said, "If you tell people to live together, and one has a desire while the other has no desire, you are telling them to quarrel."

Finally, "a healthy ear cannot stand hearing sick words." It's all up to the individual. It's up to you. If you want to achieve your dream, hang around with dreamers.

Grandma and I, preaching on the mountain, were a winning team. We trusted each other, respected each other, understood each other, and enjoyed each other.

When we got done preaching, Grandma and I prayed before we walked down from the mountain, and then we smiled at each other. Someone said, "One is not completely dressed unless one wears a smile." To me, a smile is a sign of friendliness, saying forget about the past because it has been written with disappearing ink.

Our life is defined by our beliefs. Our spirit determines how we are going to live. Freedom is the ability to decide. Conviction is defining yourself.

The final words from Grandma Miriam in September 1961, as she held my left hand, were to continue living and striving for a better life. She and I spent four days sharing and talking about her last days in this world. She said to me, "All you need to do when I die is pray for me."

I paid attention to what she was saying. These are powerful words from her heart that great achievement very often happens when our backs are up against the wall. What Grandma meant was that nothing comes from doing nothing. She said, "I know you are afraid of me dying, but know that one day we will meet in heaven." Grandma and I finally sang the last good-bye song, and that was "Nearer My God to Thee, Nearer to Thee." She stopped, and we prayed together for a long time. When she finished praying, she turned to me and called me by my middle name, Mutiso, which means "I was born when it was lightning." Grandma Miriam stated that pressure can actually enhance our performance and added that we perform when the heat is on. Finally, she said, "If you are comfortable, you may not perform." She said again that easy times don't make you better but rather slower and more complacent and sleepy. She said staying in a safety zone is dangerous.

The four days Grandma and I spent together were special days for me. The first three days, Grandma mentored me in a better way of living and gave me wisdom to pass to my kids. On the fourth day, early in the morning, Grandma said, "Mutiso, let's pray." We did, and after breakfast together, Grandma started talking again, saying, "Don't do anything that doesn't require faith." She said the key to momentum is always having something in faith to look forward to, something to anticipate. Yes, we live by faith, or we don't live at all. We either venture or vegetate.

As Grandma said, "Do not pray for easy lives. Pray to be stronger men and women."

Those four days Grandma Miriam and I spent together were the most precious time for me, even now.

I can describe Grandma like this: "When you have read the Bible, you will know it is the Word of God because you will have found it the key to your own heart, your own duty" (Woodrow Wilson).

When Grandma passed away, I was in Nairobi City and had no money to go to her funeral. I remember writing to Grandpa Mbinda, and I was crying. I remembered this from Grandpa Tumbo: "Talking with one another is loving one another." What a comfort from my heritage.

Gathering Family for Final Celebration

While I was growing up, life was different than it is now in terms of administering discipline, being committed to the family, teaching children to be brave, and getting rid of fear. We were taught that fear can affect your life and your memory. We were instructed that fear was only for cowards, and cowards could not protect families during tribal wars. Cowards had fears of death, and they were losers by tribal terms. Cowards were also the people who stole from others. Fear was not accepted in tribal life as it is accepted today.

On my dad's side, both men and women were able to predict some things ahead of time. They predicted whether we were going to have drought or plenty of rain, and so many other things. Here is the actual truth. In 1958, my grandpa Tumbo sent my grandma Mary Kamene to come get me from school. I was in my second year at Kalama Intermediate School, and I was in the sixth grade. My grandma walked twelve miles to the school and told the principal that my grandpa had sent her to get me because he knew he was dying and wanted to bless me. Grandma and I walked back home the same day. They would have sent my mom, but the tradition was that Grandma was the one who had to come to get me.

Grandma and I got home late that evening, and the tradition was that when a person was dying, the family had to kill a sheep, goat, or cow to celebrate the final living. Dad and all the others had to kill a cow, and we ate together as a family to say good-bye to Grandpa. Grandpa blessed me, out of two hundred grandkids, because I was obedient. I remember saliva all over my hands, chest, and every place. I recall his last words: "I have a hope that your family will be a blessing to many, but remember, 'A man with too much ambition cannot sleep in peace.'" This is not different from 1958; it remains the same. The people with a want and a hunger who are willing to work and be teachable will do more and gain financial freedom. If we are hungry, we are going to be in action with or without fear.

Yes, I understood the blessing part, but my only question was, why me out of two hundred grandkids? When Grandpa wanted anything done, he would ask me. Sometimes I used to ask myself why Grandpa longed for me all the time. Indeed, on his final day, as he sent Grandma Mary to come get me from school, I came to realize it was my performance for him that made the difference. I hope this can reflect for the generations of today that obedience and respect are very important, even today.

The same thing happened with Grandma Mary. When she knew she was going to die, she asked the family to walk her to her older daughter Wanza's home to die there and celebrate there.

The family took my grandma to Wanza's, and they had a sheep to kill and celebrated her last day. As I was told, she talked about me, about my obedience and willingness to do more than most people. Grandma, as I was told by my mom and aunt, told them as they were walking to Wanza's house that she missed her grandson Mutiso, but that we would meet again. She talked about my obedience and respect for others. She also told them Mutiso should have this land and that farm. Indeed, I would say I was blessed by a gracious family.

The last time I saw my father was in 1974, when my wife, Sandy, and I went to Kenya. It was Sandy's first time in Africa. Sandy used to ask me what kind of houses we had lived in growing up in Kenya. I used to joke by telling her that we lived in huts and had elevators to get on top of the huts. Well, she believed it until she got to Kenya and saw for herself the way we had lived.

In June 1974, we flew from Minneapolis, Minnesota, to New York City. This was a blessing to me. I happened to have a seat next to Harry Belafonte, and he and I talked all the way to New York. Harry Belafonte said he had been in Kenya and it was such a beautiful country.

I saw my dad and mom in the country, and then they came to see us in Nairobi City. Here is something I do not expect anyone to understand. My gracious dad said to me, "Son, Mutiso, this is our last day for you and I to see each other in this life." This is a fact: Two days before my dad's death, I told Sandy I was going to get a call from Kenya that someone close to me was dying. This was in June 1975. Well, in two days I received a telegram that my dad had passed away in the evening.

I was then going to law school full time and working full time. I had no money to fly to my dad's funeral. The week I received the telegram, I went to my bank and talked to the bank vice president. I had never met him before. A loving man was sent to me during a time of great need. This gentleman said, "I understand your situation. I will be your guarantor. I will loan you the four thousand dollars, and you should pay it within six months."

I got the funds, but my passport had been expired for five years. I called the Kenyan embassy in New York, and they told me it would take two weeks for my passport to be renewed. I have been a risk taker all my life. I flew to Kenya without a renewed passport. At the airport when I arrived, I had six hundred people waiting for me. I had so many challenges at the airport, but I knew there would be an answer in the end.

Here is the amazing thing for me and for those six hundred people who met me at the Nairobi airport. As I was trying to resolve the challenges, I heard someone speaking in my mother's tongue, and I went and talked to him about the problems I was having entering the country. The man behind the counter had been trying to charge me exorbitant fees as a way of grabbing some extra money for himself. This man went and settled it for me, and I was finally free to leave and be with the people who were waiting for me.

I stayed in Nairobi City with friends, and the following day my cousin gave me a ride to my dad's funeral. More than two thousand people were there, and I did not know many of them.

According to the culture, I was bound to be at Dad's final celebration, and I was the first to speak. I wrote the speech for my dad's final celebration, and when I finished people were crying because of the way I put everything together.

Here is what my cousin who was in the same hospital with my dad told me and other people. Dad came to him and said, "One of us will go home, and the other person will have a final celebration and joy." In two days, Dad was gone.

I remember a lot of things about my dad, who was so detailed I used to tease him that he would know when flies died. Dad told us to tell everyone in his family not to worry about anything because worry affects your joy of life and diminishes enjoyment of life. I found a quote that fit my dad's belief not to worry: "Worry does not contribute to life. It takes away from life. Worry is a thief. It robs us of our time, diminishes enjoyment, and reduces the quality of the present moment. At our journey's end, we may look back and realize that every hour spent worrying was a precious gift thrown away. To worry is to steal from one's self" (David L. Weatherford).

Urgency of Going to See Mom

In 1998 I had a sense of urgency to go see my mom in Kenya after twenty-four years. I flew from Minneapolis, Minnesota, to Chicago, Illinois, and then to London. From London I flew by KLM to the Sultanate of Oman, then to Nairobi. The flight from Minneapolis to Kenya took seventeen hours. Yes. You get five days of jet lag.

I got to the airport and was waiting for my baggage. One of the customs officials at the airport saw the camera I was carrying and told me I had to pay duty on it. When I asked why, he said it was a policy. I was speaking in English, and he thought I was from the United States. Beside this man was another gentleman whom I heard speaking in my Kamba tribe language. I turned and said "Hi" in the Kamba language, and he responded "Hi" to me. I asked him why I had to pay duty for the camera. He asked me who wanted to charge for duty. I said the other gentleman. Both men started talking in Swahili, which I also understood very well. Then the man who spoke my Kamba dialect said I was good to go. We will face challenges, but we have to be calm and positive.

This was two in the afternoon on a Saturday. This time, going to see my mom and the family, I told them not to tell people I was coming for a visit. Well, in spite of my request, about two hundred people were waiting for me at the airport. I took all two hundred people to the Railways Restaurant and fed them all. We had the food of the soul, talking and laughing. My parents taught us to be givers, not takers. I had four big boxes full of used clothing, and each person picked up what he wanted. Of course, we all wore different sizes of clothes. Some people found what fit them, and some didn't. Amazingly, we had a great time at the Railways Restaurant. I picked out the restaurant because I used to work for East African Railways, which in those days included Kenya, Tanzania, and Uganda.

My daughter Aline had a graduation that month. I did not want to miss it, but she said, "You need to go see Grandma because it's very important to you and to the family."

As a close family, we spent three weeks having the food of the soul, as Grandpa used to call it. One day, the whole family was eating at noon at a restaurant in Nairobi City, and Mom started speaking to the family. As was our tradition when the elders started speaking, everyone listened, and no one was to interrupt. Mom stopped for a moment and said one of Grandpa's proverbs, "Copying everybody else all the time, the monkey one day cut his throat." With a big smile, Mom said to my brothers and sisters, "We all should thank God for your brother Mutiso. He has been driven to achieve all his life." She stopped, and her tears started dropping. We gave her some tissue to wipe her tears away.

She started telling a story about when I was five years old. I was very sick. She told the family that she carried me on her back for nine miles to catch a bus to a private doctor in Machatos, twenty-three miles away. When she and I got to this private doctor, he examined me and told Mom I had a heart with a hole. Mom stopped again, and the tears were coming down like a flood. Indeed, the doctor said I would not live long. Mom paid the doctor and carried me to catch the bus home. Mom and I got home, and she told my two grandmas, Miriam and Mary, what the doctor had told her about me. Mom said, "When one is troubled, one remembers God." Grandmas Miriam and Mary had a strong faith. Mom told the family that my grandmas prayed and prayed for me. My grandmas' prayers were answered, and I am still here with you. I had never heard the story until that day. I was too young to remember.

Gracious Mom continued telling my brothers and sisters, "You don't have to do as your brother Mutiso has done all his life supporting the entire family, but now he has his own family." She told my brothers and sisters, "You have to depend on yourselves, not your brother." Mom asked them, "If your brother is called home, where will you get support?" You should have heard the silence. It was an emotional day.

The following day, I had to leave for South Africa because my mentor and friend, Bert Gulick, had asked me to go out there to do a seminar. I had never been to South Africa before, but we had sent my son, Phil, there to build a business when he was about twenty years old.

I remember the day I told Phil's mom that I was sending him to South Africa to build our business. She said, "Why are you sending a twenty-year-old kid to a country he has never been to and where he does not know anyone?" My response was that I had come to the United States at almost the same age, and I knew no one at all. I was taught not to fear dangerous animals and many other things. I was taught that brave people don't quit, but that cowards quit and cannot be responsible for protecting women during tribal wars. I was taught to live with a purpose in life. Indeed, be purpose driven to touch others in business, ministry, mentoring, or whatever you do. Do everything with excitement. Phil did a great job. Phil learned how to build financial freedom as I have done for years. As my grandpa said, "He who does not cultivate his field will die of hunger." I recommend you to cultivate your faith and financial freedom if you have a desire and are willing to work hard to achieve.

I had a great time in South Africa for a week, and then I returned to Kenya.

While I was in Kenya, Mom and I got together, and we talked and laughed. One day Mom said, "Your son who has a middle name like Grandpa's is special like you." She was talking about Phil. Mom said, "My grandson Phil, when he came to Kenya with his sister, gave me this and that, and I blessed him to be wealthy."

African tradition on blessings is very important. Obedience is important. In the Kamba tribe, the blessings begin when you are born. As you grow, parents and grandparents watch your obedience. If you are asked to go look after livestock and you complain in a certain way, the elders know. If you are asked to go get something from the neighbors and they were never told ahead of time that you would be coming to pick it up, if you act in a bad way, even if you do what you have been asked to do, your blessings are lessened. How you treat others each day is watched.

The way kids who are smart learn whether their blessings are in order is by noticing when the elders kill a goat, sheep, or cow. The head of a cow, goat, or sheep gets cooked and then reserved for the elders to eat together in the morning. All the kids in the village can come, too. The elders already know the obedient kids and the disobedient ones. During this time, the elders don't want any kids to understand what they are saying, so they communicate by talking in signs. One elder will tell another elder whom to give the meat to and whom not to give the meat to.

Also, as you grow up and start supporting parents and grandparents, it is a blessing for you.

If you don't really understand blessing, read the Bible. Jacob was wrestling with an angel to bless him. The angel said, "Blessed Jacob, let me go." Mind you, thieves never get blessed at all.

The culture has a strong belief that if you are not blessed, life never turns out well. When there is a blessing in the village, you can tell because elders come wearing blankets, and you can tell the joy they have by watching their faces. I knew all this because my grandparents all blessed me. All that I know about blessing comes from the times I watched it done on what the Kamba tribe called a temple of spirit. It was the largest tree and had a large shade with a huge trunk. I went with elders in the village and watched them blessing the people who had passed away.

When they got to the temple of spirit, they made a fire and killed a goat or sheep to celebrate the ones who were good people by obedience and by treating others well no matter what they were going through that day.

When they began the ceremony, they kept silent for almost half an hour, and you could not hear any noise except birds singing. When they began mentioning the people who had passed away, with each man giving blessing to them, all you could hear was "mmm" in response to the person who was blessing the ones who did good for others. The elders each dropped a piece of meat on the temple of spirit. What I was amazed by was that no one ever said at the blessing, "You are wrong." The elders were so uniform in the way they communicated.

Here is my final conclusion about my mom, dad, and grandparents from an anonymous quotation I found: "Courage does not always roar; sometimes courage is the quiet voice at the end of the day saying, 'I will try again tomorrow.'"

In America, you can be anything you want to be. America is the best in the world, and that's why you see people coming to America or dying at sea trying. We have to create a dream to work for. I am afraid to say, when people say money is the root of all evil, they don't understand the Bible at all. I tell them, "Just bring all the roots to me, and I will be rich and financially free serving other people."

I respect Zig Ziglar, who used to say, "You will get all you want in life if you help enough other people get what they want."

Most of us have so much on our plates because we take everything that comes to us. The statement that I can only expose you to is, "I am so busy doing nothing that I can't do anything else." If that is all we want, who can mentor us to change? It's only you and me.

Flying Back to the United States

The time came to come back home on June 21, 1998. At the airport, nine people were waiting to say good-bye to me, including my mom. My mom pulled me aside and spoke to me very softly. "Mutiso, will you and your family ever come back to live in Kenya?"

I leaned over and said, "Mom, I don't think I will ever come back to live here again, but I will come to visit."

My dear, gracious mom leaned to me and said, "You have a beautiful family. You have supported us since you were twelve years old, and you have done so while you have been in the United States for thirty-three years." Mom was the first to mentor me, and she could tell that I had never lost the way I was taught about respecting my elders. Again, she started using the proverbs we grew up with. She said, "When a heart overflows, it comes out through the mouth." Then Mom said, "This is the last time you and I will see each other." So for my mom and me, our last day of living celebration was June 21, 1998. That day, I gave money to my mom, my brother, and my two sisters. I hugged everyone good-bye and walked to the gate to catch my plane.

When I got to the gate, four police officers were waiting. They looked at my passport and asked for my proof of permanent residency in the United States. They looked at it and said, "You are living in the United States illegally." I told them I had been in the United States for thirty-three years.

If you get to know me, you will see I believe I can handle anything by prayer. I told the police officers to call the American embassy. They did, and the American embassy told them they had never seen my residency papers because I had been in the United States for thirty-three years. The American embassy told the police to let me go back home to the United States.

My flight had been delayed for forty-five minutes, and I got cleared in Kenya to come home. We flew to the Sultanate of Oman and got there at about nine thirty at night. They started calling people to get on a bus to drive to their flights. We all got in line to be checked so we could ride on the bus. I got to the gate, and they told me to go and sit down. I went and sat down, and I heard a man speaking my national language, Swahili. I went to him, and I told him my story about living in the United States. He called the American embassy and was told I had been living in the United States legally for thirty-three years. So the bus took me to catch the plane to Dubai and to the United States.

The plane landed at the Dubai airport at midnight. Amazingly, two guys wearing white uniforms came on the plane and said three people on the plane were living in the United States illegally. Immediately, they started checking everyone's passports. They took with them three passports, including mine. They got off the plane and waited for half an hour. The two uniformed men then came back and gave me back my passport and gave a second man back his passport. The two uniformed men took with them a seventy-two-year-old man. How did I know the man was seventy-two years old? Because they asked him if he was seventy-two years old, and he said yes.

We took off from the Dubai airport, and I closed my eyes to talk to God. I talked to Him on and off for six hours. We flew all night. On June 22, 1998, we landed at the Chicago airport during the day.

As always in American airports, when flights come in from other countries, there is a line for noncitizens and a line for American citizens. Not being an American citizen, I mistakenly went to the line where American citizens were. They checked everyone's passport. They looked at my passport, and I immediately asked them if I was in the wrong line. Their response was, "You have been in the United States for thirty-three years, and now is the time for you to become a US citizen." A police officer took me to a room to fill out an application to become an American citizen. The police officer told me that when I got to Minneapolis I should take the application to Immigration, and they would set up an interview for citizenship. Decide what you want in life and work for it; anything free is worthless because you did not work for it.

In 1999, I finally became an American citizen. I am proud to be an American. If you read *Acres of Diamonds*, you will find that people were looking for diamonds. And so did I in coming to the United States longing for an education. Note this: I came to the United States looking for diamonds, and I got the education I wanted, all with scholarships from high school through college. I had to pay my way only in law school.

I came from Kenya looking for acres of diamonds, and I found my diamonds in meeting Dan and Betsy, who sponsored us in the Amway business. They showed me a way to do more by finding people who are so ambitious and hungry that they cannot sleep in peace because they want their dream so badly and are willing to earn it with action. Dan and Betsy led me to more "acres of diamonds" by exposing me to Bert and Jackie, Jerry and Cherry, Dwight and Margaret Ann, Tony and Sue, and Dex and Birdie. These people are the line of my sponsors and mentors.

If you have not read the book *Acres of Diamonds*, read it. Dex and Birdie have touched thousands and thousands of people around the world because they had the dream to build the business and not quit. Be moved by your dream and willing to work for it, and you will see amazing results.

Sometimes I ask myself, *What if I had given up struggling to come to the United States because of the setbacks I faced? What would my life be today?* I hate to think about it. I am so glad today for what my grandparents and parents taught me—that cowards quit when things get hard, but the brave with incessant dreams stick with what they start, no matter what. Cowards do nothing except tear things apart, and that is why my tribe won't allow them to protect the women.

Aim so high you will never be bored. The greatest waste of our natural resources is the number of people who never achieve their potential. Get out of that slow lane. Shift into that fast lane. If you think you can't, you won't. If you think you can, there is a good chance you will. Even making the effort will make you feel like a new person. Reputations are made by searching for things that cannot be done and doing them. "Aim low: boring. Aim high: soaring."

First Family Visit to Kenya

The hardest part of missing friends is not their absence; it is when you think of all those good times and ask yourself, "Will those moments ever happen again?"

I had the courage and drive to go to school in the United States at Augustana Academy. The goals I had—and accomplished—were to complete high school in two years and complete my bachelor's degree at Augustana College with majors in business administration, economics, and sociology. Yes, I also worked, even though I had a full scholarship for four years at Augustana Academy and Augustana College. I thank both the academy and Augustana College for helping me and for providing good professors like the late Dr. Elliot Thorson, Dr. Les Carlson, Dr. K. Bourg, and the late Paul Agger. They were great professors and were my gracious friends. They were with me during my challenges, and they could tell when I was in class. I am a deep and analytical thinker, and all my professors encouraged me.

I remember in economics class, Dr. Carlson said the words "no man's land" one day. I did not understand what he was talking about. I just let it go, and when I got home I went to the dictionary to find the meaning of "no man's land." I could not find it. The following day, we had economics class again. I always sat in the front row. I raised my hand to find out the meaning of "no man's land." I told Dr. Carlson that I had looked in the dictionary for "no man's land" and could not find it. Well, the whole class laughed so hard, but they were my friends. Dr. Carlson said, "Mr. Isika, it's American slang."

"The number one reason people give up so quickly is that they tend to look at how far they still have to go instead of how far they have gotten."

After seven years in the United States, I had completed high school and college. It was time to go see my parents and others back home. I had come to the United States with a small, green suitcase, and in it I had one black suit and two sets of underwear. Going back to Kenya for a visit, I had my wife, Sandy, and our daughter, Aline. Aline was four months old. Today, Aline remains a special daughter and has grown into a beautiful lady who is very detailed and goal oriented.

It was July 1974 when we flew from Minneapolis, Minnesota, to New York. It was the first time Sandy had been to New York. In New York, we stayed with my friend, Professor Makau, who had also been my seventh-grade math teacher in Kenya. The following day, we flew from New York to Brussels, Belgium, and then to Kampala, Uganda. We landed in Kampala at three in the morning. I got out of the plane to get something to drink and left Sandy on the plane with Aline. Within ten minutes, Sandy came to the airport carrying Aline. It was very dangerous in those days. It was by the grace of God that she did not get kidnapped.

At the airport I bought a can of pop. I gave them a five-dollar bill and asked for change a couple of times with no response. A gentleman sitting at the other end came and told me not to ask for change. "You will be kidnapped," he said. This is the way they make a living now.

I said to the gentleman, "Thank you for saving my life."

Within five minutes, they announced that the flight going to Kenya would be leaving in forty-five minutes. We boarded the plane. We got to the Nairobi airport about ten in the morning.

Surprisingly, a few people came to the Nairobi airport to meet us. All of them were so excited to see every one of us. When we left the airport, we all went to eat at a restaurant. Most of the people who had come to meet us knew me, and they told stories about me going to Sunday school for three years without missing a day. They talked about me not quitting school like the other kids from my village. They talked about my cousin and I throwing away our books and walking thirty miles to work for Indians in Konza and how we came home with our clothes all black because we had cooked with charcoal. They talked about how I had refused to sing "God Bless the Queen" and got suspended from school several times.

During this time, one person spoke as if he knew my faith. He said, "The plan God had for Mutiso was not for comfort but to continue pursuing more and more for God and for the things God calls him for." He said that if we are comfortable where we are, we will be lost.

There was much joking and laughter as people told different stories about me. All the time these stories were being told, I was just tired from flying for twenty-four hours, with a six-hour layover in London.

One of the men knew me when I worked for East African Railways. He stood up and said that Mutiso follows rules that are written down. He said that when he was a guard, or train conductor, on the trains, the general manager brought his car to be loaded on a train when I was in charge. The general manager, who was traveling with the presidents of five countries, came and talked to me about not having papers to get his car on the train.

As low a position as I had, I knew the law, and I told him to go get the document before I would load his car on a train I was in charge of. In short, I delayed the five presidents for two hours. When I returned home, my name was all over the *East African Standard* with so much negativity about me delaying presidents for two hours at the Nairobi railway station. At any rate, I was suspended for three months with pay. I was called into court to explain the situation. I won the case and was called back to resume my duties as a train guard. When we believe who we are and pursue our dreams, we will face challenges, and we need to find someone we can talk with about our situation. When I received this suspension, I talked to people I trusted and had a great relationship with. Life is all about relationships.

That evening at the restaurant, people started to fight about who was going to take us to the place where we were going to stay that night. Finally, my cousin took us in his car. It was quite an experience, after being away from home for seven years and having brought my family with me, to see how loving and caring the people were. The truth is, there was no negativity at the gathering. As Grandpa Tumbo said, "A healthy ear cannot stand hearing sick words."

The first night, we stayed with a friend of mine who was in charge of the Game Reserve. Because Sandy had never been on a Game Reserve safari, my friend gave his driver instructions to take us to the Nairobi Game

Reserve to see the wildlife. We saw all kinds of animals. We were warned to not open the car doors and to stay inside all the time. The warning was the danger you can face when you open the car door or get out of the car. All kinds of monkeys were around the car, and some were on the car. The driver said that if you run over one of the monkeys, you are put in jail for six months.

The second day, my cousin Daniel Mbai came and picked us up, and we stayed at their home in Limuru.

The third day, my cousin said they were raising school funds in Nzaini village. My cousin said we were going to drive my white Toyota. The car was packed with four adults, two kids, and chickens. We drove to the fundraising on Saturday.

When we got there, many people were there, and more were still on the way. My cousin was instructed by my clan and others to leave Sandy and Aline in the car and take it back outside the village gate. I was instructed to walk behind the car with respect. As we got outside the gate, two dancing clans came with bright clothes and ornaments around their necks, legs, and arms. These dancing ornaments made beautiful sounds.

As was the tradition, my cousin now began to drive into the village through the gate. I was walking behind the car. Some of the women had brooms made from tree branches, and they wiped the outside of the car from the back and both sides. All four clans were singing, "Mutiso, you are welcome home, and your family is welcome home." This went on for fifteen minutes.

By two o'clock in the afternoon, my cousin Daniel and the mayor, Nelson Kavuti, began the fundraising.

First they introduced me to everyone because some of the people had never heard of me. They didn't know me because when I was growing up I was a focused kid set on accomplishing what I had to do. Mayor Kavuti knew me because he was my teacher in grade school.

Through all of this, I was thinking, *where are these people going to get money from?* Since I had left, nothing much had changed. I was right, because the funds that were raised that day were very little.

After the welcome of me and my family, the mayor, and my cousin Daniel Mbai, four tribes wearing bright clothes sang and danced.

The first clan was singing and playing drums and blowing whistles. They were singing and mentioning my name, Mutiso from Tumbo's family, and mentioning how different I was from other kids growing up, obedient and with a mind-set to accomplish things. They were dancing and shaking their shoulders back and forth. The clothes they wore had red, brown, black, green, and other colors. They started dancing around me and Sandy and Aline. I remember one song they sang was to come home and lead us in the village of Nzaini.

The other three clans all came in dancing, as well. They wore bright colors of tribal clothes made of cotton. They wore dancing cloths that matched the red of the soil. The three clans sang in turns, playing drums and shaking their shoulders back and forth. This time they had singing about welcoming me and my family, and they said, "Mutiso, you are loved, you are loved." As they sang, I interpreted for Sandy what they were saying in their music.

At the end, the mayor said, "Now we are welcoming people to donate money for the school." We watched people donate money in Kenyan shillings, and we were the last to donate funds. We went up but donated very little—800 shillings—because we were both going to graduate school at the time. The mayor told the people how much we had donated, and he said we had donated more than everyone else combined.

I had won many contests, such as track events, debates, and soccer games, but I hadn't seen anyone celebrate about me like these four Kamba clans. Being welcomed home was fabulous and inspiring for me and Sandy. What was amazing for me was all four clans singing, dancing, and playing drums. The celebration was on me. Really, I never thought that anyone would honor me. At the end, five people went in front to sing "Nearer My God to Thee, Nearer to Thee." They sang in my language. I remember Sandy saying, "I never knew how much you had done in life until I went with you to Kenya and saw the respect people had for you."

Grandpa said, "When spider webs unite, they can tie up a lion."

Visiting Kenya was a life-giving renewal for me because I never thought of people celebrating me or my family. We were next to nothing in the Nzaini village, even though my parents were servants of others. I will repeat Grandpa's way of seeing things, as he said, "If relatives help each other, what evil can hurt them?" No evil can hurt a team that has a dream, knows Jesus, and doesn't dwell on wrongs. The only people who never do anything wrong are dead.

"The fool is thirsty in the midst of water." Who knew when I was growing up in a family that had love but no material things that people would celebrate me and my family? It is all about having a dream and being in action, not merely talking about what we might do.

Again, the clans started singing and mentioning my name and Grandpa Tumbo's name. It was interesting that during the day's events, the women took our daughter with them for more than three hours. For three hours, we did not see Aline, and we did not worry about her. I trusted the women, knowing how much they appreciated children. When the fundraising was over, Mayor Kavuti said, "We knew Mutiso was going to be something because he never took anything for granted."

That evening we drove back to Nairobi City and stayed again with my cousin. My cousin and his family did not have a crib for Aline, so she had to sleep in the suitcase we traveled with.

Traveling in Kenya

One morning, we went to have breakfast in Nairobi City Center, and as we were placing orders, I turned to Sandy and told her not to eat a lot. She asked why, and I told her that all day we would be visiting friends and relatives, and they would feed us in every home we went to. I told her if she didn't taste their food, it was considered rude in our tradition. That day, we went to eight homes, and we tasted everything. We tasted smashed beans, white corn, cassava, millet, homemade bread, cabbage greens, and much more.

Because I had been a train conductor for four years, we decided to travel by train, first class, to a city called Nakuru. There, more than two thousand flamingos lived at Lake Nakuru. We stayed in a nice hotel, and the following day we rented a car to go to Lake Nakuru to see the flamingos. We were instructed to stay on the path and follow each other. They told us if we got off of the path we would sink to our deaths. We enjoyed it immensely.

We did not stay in Nakuru long. After visiting the flamingo village, we caught a train to Mombasa. On this train I met a classmate. We had sat at the same desk from fifth grade to eighth grade. I sat on the right side, and he sat on the left side. Both of us had been good in math and English.

We traveled all night. Sandy and Aline got sick on the train that night. It was an experience for me to have two people throwing up on the train and have no choice but to watch. The train arrived at the Mombasa railway station at nine in the morning. I had not slept all night because I had two sick people to watch. My friend said good-bye and told us he would come the following day to visit with us. He did, and we had a fabulous time talking about our time in school playing soccer, volleyball, and other such things.

Before we left Mombasa, I took Sandy and Aline to see Fort Jesus, which was built by Portuguese pirates for protection. It is like a rock; you can bomb it and nothing will happen to it. Being in Mombasa, I had great memories because after I had completed my training at RTS, I was sent to work there. My classmate at RTS, Paul Wambere, and I lived in the same junky house in Kibarani, and each morning we had to walk or catch a city bus.

Again, I love traveling and meeting people. Mombasa is a fun place to be because it is on the Indian Ocean. One year Phil and Aline visited their grandma in Kenya and went to Mombasa to swim in the ocean. They called us in the evening and talked about how clean the water was.

After visiting Fort Jesus, we took a cab to Nairobi City, 330 miles away. It cost us 2,500 shillings in Kenyan money. That is thirty-three dollars in American money. When traveling back, we were in the center of wildlife. We saw along the way all kinds of animals, such as elephants, zebras, leopards, you name it.

When we got to Nairobi City, we traveled on a city bus because cars were limited. One thing I appreciated when we traveled on buses was that men always stood up, leaving their seats to allow Sandy and Aline to sit down.

"Celebrate the good life with the people you love." Before we left Kenya for home, Mom and Dad came to see us. For Dad, it was the last time to say good-bye to me and my family.

"The best gift you could ever give someone is your time, because you are giving them something that you will never get back" (www.livelifehappy.com).

It was enjoyable for my parents to see me and my family. I appreciate that the people who put up with you on your darkest nights are the ones worth spending your brightest days with. My parents saw many defeating days for me, but I refused to surrender to setbacks. I persist with actions. You do not have to have passion, but just a dream to achieve by telling your story. The people who say no to your storytelling are the ones about whom Grandpa used to say, "A person who does not travel says his mother cooks the best food."

America, wake up and start seeing opportunities instead of staying home and just working for others for forty-five years or more, if you are lucky. Home and work for so many years is just milking a bull without milk. Think big.

Our time visiting Kenya came to an end, and we returned to the United States. I did not want to be a citizen at that time because I had a dream to be a politician and the president. I was warned by so many people that I am too honest and wouldn't last long. Yes, I would love to live more than a hundred years. My family and I returned to our loving country, the United States, from Nairobi via Athens, Greece, and we continued working and going to law school.

Down the road you will hear more stories about how I went to my classmate's twenty-ninth birthday party and met an interesting couple. The husband asked where I came from, and my story took more than an hour to tell.

Once you make a decision, the universe conspires to make it happen if you have a want that is bad enough and if you want to be mentored.

Coming to America with only an eighth-grade education was not luck, but a relationship with God, which is the most important relationship you can have. Embrace it every day.

4

Financial Freedom

Inspiration

Going to Nzaini to raise school funds and hearing Nelson Kavuti speak gave me inspiration. He spoke about how I had repeated first grade and ended up not quitting school as did the other kids. When we give up, what is the alternative? Giving up is an excuse. I repeat it as Grandpa Tumbo said, "I have a cow in the sky but cannot drink her milk." I may fail several times and learn from it, but I will never give up on continuing what I like to do and giving it freely to other people. My advice to those who want badly to touch other people's lives is to know your mission, and you will never be bothered by negatives from others.

Our future has nothing to do with the past. Again, the past has been written with disappearing ink.

I always had the courage not to surrender my future by listening to discouragements from others. God sends us someone to show us an opportunity, but we think opportunity is hard work. Mind you, anything we get for free we don't appreciate much because we never worked for it. For example, why do healthy, able people waste away their lives? Why in America do we have some people who don't want to go to work but depend on government support instead? It is not that they are bad people, but they don't have a dream to work and achieve the life they could have.

Remember that "the opportunity God sends does not wake up who is asleep." We fall asleep because we don't want badly enough to achieve our dream. I have a goal in a few years to fly to Kenya four times a year. I came to the United States with only forty-five dollars.

My final word is that if you have dreams, and you are willing to work and be coachable, don't follow a blind man or woman who has no dreams. Let's set an example for our family by working on what we want.

Opportunity Footprints

The best way to predict the future is to create it, but don't spend too much time on yesterday, because yesterday has been written with disappearing ink.

America was developed on the principles of free enterprise by people who had dreams. Those individuals did not put periods on their failures. They had one question in their minds: "What is the next larger thing?" Precisely, what are the next dreams and goals? They wrote them down, and they put dates for achieving what they set out to achieve.

I have found that you cannot win until you are not afraid to lose. We need to coach the current generation about loving and caring and about dreams and wanting them badly enough to work hard for them. Dreamers create their financial freedom and are willing to work hard when others view hard work in a negative way.

Each day I am thankful for nights that turn into mornings, friends that turn into family, dreams that turn into reality, and likes that turn into love.

In 1976, I was a junior executive with a large corporation. I was working hard, long hours. Every day when I sat at that desk, I felt as if I were in jail in those cubes with no windows. Going back and forth between home and work each day was not my dream at all. Being in America, the greatest country on earth and the land of free enterprise, I was interested in associating with people who had businesses. This is important: when you want something badly enough that you think about it all the time, then you have a dream to go after.

One day, I came home from work and told Sandy that we were going to the Marriott Inn on Friday and Saturday and would return Sunday. We took yellow writing pads with us. That weekend we wrote down our dreams and goals. There were no ifs or buts, just dreams, goals, dates, and actions.

Finding Acres of Diamonds

A week later, one of my classmates in law school had his twenty-ninth birthday, and he invited us to the party. I am not a party person, but I had to go to this one. It was on a Friday evening. More than fifty people were there, most of them law students and practicing attorneys.

A gentleman with red hair was there with his wife. This gentleman introduced himself and his wife to us. He was polite and positive. The four of us sat together while the rest of the party went to another room to have the food of the soul (just to talk and have fun). This man's name was Dan Smith. He asked me where I came from. I told him that I came from Kenya. Then he asked, "What brought you to the United States?" It took an hour for me to explain how and why I had come. Little did I know he was interviewing me to see whether I would qualify to be his business associate. After I finished telling him my story, he concluded that I had a good attitude and that I had dreams. When you want something badly, you find a way to achieve it. Dan was a salesman, and I was a transportation analyst in the same company. We lived about eight blocks from each other. All this time Dan and I were getting to know each other, Betsy and Sandy were listening.

After we got done talking, Dan gave me his business card. I had learned during the colonial days that Europeans with red hair were the ones who were rude to Kenyans, but as we parted, Dan asked me to call him so that he could show me a business idea we could do together.

All my life I have communicated with God in prayers, and I do it three to four times a day or more. I went to pray for this, but I knew God had a purpose for me. How could this happen when Sandy and I had just been to the

Marriott Inn to write our dreams and goals? Be open to listen and hear the voice of God.

I went by myself to see the marketing plan at his house. Dan gave me a book by Rich DeVos called *Believe* and two tapes to listen to. I put everything he gave me under the bed and forgot about reading the book and listening to the tapes. Today we listen to CDs for continuing education, and it is up to each individual to decide whether he or she want to subscribe.

As a follow-through, Dan called me back and said he wanted to show the marketing plan to Sandy. My response was that in Kenya women don't go into business with their husbands. Dan's response was that in this business we need our wives. Dan and Betsy came to our home and showed the marketing plan to me and Sandy. Sandy got excited to get the business going. Indeed, we got started with the Amway business as independent business owners.

Anne Frank said, "No one has ever become poor by giving." So find something you like to do and spend your life giving it away to people.

In the Amway business, we show the marketing plan to those who are looking. Those who see the marketing plan and say no will never remember us. But those who say yes will never forget us. We are loving givers, and that is all we do—give, give, give. The greatest challenge is to find someone who knows all your flaws, differences, and mistakes and yet still sees the best in you. That is Dan, Betsy, and Sandy.

That evening, Dan and Betsy shared the full marketing plan the second time. We got excited to build our Amway business. They suggested that we come to a rally in Ames,

Iowa. It was a five-hour drive. Sandy had to work that weekend, so I had to go. Dan and Betsy drove their red car, and I rode with them.

We got to Ames, and the host was Dwight Smith, who used to ask me, "Nick, how are you?"

My response used to be, "Better than the average bear." I hate average because the average individuals pretend that they sleep in peace, but they sleep in frustration.

Mark this and do more research: the people who are beyond average because they want to make a difference in others' lives don't go to sleep in peace because they are thinking of whom they can contact to show people how to achieve what they want. We cannot follow someone else's dream but only our own.

At any rate, I got to the function, which they called a rally, and the hosts, Dwight and Margaret Smith, got on stage and introduced Jerry and Cherry Meadows. People clapped and made a lot of noise. I did not sit with Dan and Betsy, but I sat in my own area. I have had fun building my Amway business. At that rally, fifteen hundred white people with three thousand eyes were looking at one black guy who had nothing. I am a man of wanting badly, and I don't like wishers because wishers will slaughter America step by step, and America will be left empty and wishing.

At that rally, I made up my mind to build the Amway business. After the business-development seminar was over, Dan introduced me to Jerry and Cherry. That evening we all stayed at Dan's parents' home. Sandy and I did not have much to put into the business, but we got going. When I got done with my law exams, I started to build the business with only two days a week, on Saturday and Sunday after church. I traveled to some towns in Minnesota where they had never seen a black person. I think some people thought I was from Mars. I was always friendly to people because I love working with people.

The reason most foreigners come into the Amway business as independent business owners is that someone came to their home to show them an opportunity. In fact, most of these foreigners don't like being controlled paycheck to paycheck. They like being with people and sharing.

Dale Carnegie said, "People rarely succeed unless they have fun in what they are doing." Being a foreigner, I could not see being at a job for many years, but I always dreamed of being my own boss. Success is not easy, but it is much better than regret down the road.

Too many people want to bargain the price of success. What we think all day is what we become, so protect your thoughts.

One person can start the wave in the Amway business and touch a lot of people's lives. Of course, some people will laugh at you and tell you ignorant things. What I have learned is that ignorance has no defense. If anyone laughs when you are building your financial future, remember what my grandpa used to tell those people: "When a mouse laughs at the cat, there is a hole nearby."

The point I want to make is to do something besides your day job so that you don't have regrets at the end. It is not only for money but also for touching others' lives, and the change is much better than money.

Each successful person has a painful story to tell. Each painful story has a successful ending. Accept the pain, achieve the benefit. Indeed, that's real life.

Here is the point made by Tony Gaskins: "If you don't build your dream, someone will hire you to build theirs."

Michael Altshuler supports Tony Gaskins by saying it another way. Here is Michael Altshuler's final statement: "The bad news is time flies. The good news is you're the pilot."

In your life and mine, we are going to face negatives, but never put a period on a negative thought. Coming to the United States, I faced many negatives, but I continued to pursue my dream. Today I am a full citizen. I don't even remember the people who discouraged me, but I remember the ones who encouraged me.

In any networking you will find that some people come into your life and quickly go. Some stay for a while and leave footprints in our lives and on our hearts. And we are never the same. All along the way, I have told people on my team that if others are dumb enough to walk away, be smart enough to let them go.

We appreciate Dan and Betsy because they gave us an opportunity to start our own business, and along with that opportunity came a mentor with an educational system that taught:

1. People skills.
2. Communication skills.
3. Leadership skills.

The mentor fulfilled for us as adults the role my grandfather provided to me as a child: an introduction to principles and guidance for implementing those principles in my life. Success is all endeavor and is based upon the adoption of universal principles.

The mentoring and education have affected my abilities as an employee, a businessman, a husband, and a father, and they continue to this day.

Finally, the most beautiful people we have known are those who take their time to share an opportunity with others as Dan and Betsy did with us.

Thomas Edison said it right: "Opportunity is missed by most people because it is dressed in overalls and looks like work."

If you change nothing in your life, nothing will change.

Never think about the past, but think about the future and be driven by the future to achieve what you want.

Going to the Augustana Academy full time, I also worked full time in a factory one mile from the school. After school ended at three o'clock, I had to go to work for eight hours. I did it wintertime and summertime. When you and I have dreams, facts mean nothing, or they don't count at all.

Meeting the Corey Family

In the summer, I lived at the academy dorms by myself. During summer after work, I came back to the dormitory to take a shower and change clothes. Every evening for a month, I walked past a particular home. One evening, as I was walking to downtown Canton to eat dinner, four kids, all brothers and sisters, were outside this home. One of the girls said, "Hey, black man, how come your face is dirty?" I stopped to talk to the four kids. I asked their names. We talked with great smiles.

The four-year-old kid said before I left, "Hey, black man, next time wash your face to get rid of the black dirt." I was the only black person in town.

The next evening, I walked past the same house, and the four kids were outside on their porch. They saw me walking, and they all waved at me. The four-year-old said, "Hey, black man, you did not wash your face to get rid of the dirt." She asked me if she could touch my face.

I said, "Yes, Caroline."

Grandpa Tumbo said, "Talking with one another is loving one another." I leaned down for Caroline to touch my face. She touched it and was trying to clean up the black dirt, but the black dirt did not come off my face. I tried to explain it when her brother and two sisters were there. I told her that my color is black, and it is the way I will be my entire life.

Grandpa said, "He who begins a conversation does not foresee the end."

After I had talked to the four kids two or three times, they talked to their parents about me. Grandpa used to say, "A borrowed fiddle does not furnish a tune." One evening, the kids saw me walking in front of their home, and they told me to wait. Bob Corey, the father, came and met me, and his wife, Connie, was beside him.

The first question Bob asked me was, "Where are you from?"

I said, "From Kenya, East Africa." You should have seen their faces. It was such a big surprise to see a young lad from a far continent who had come to America all by himself. They invited me to come for supper over the weekend. That weekend, I was with the family for four hours. It was the beginning of a great friendship because Bob and Connie liked me very much. So every weekend that summer I was with the whole family eating at their home. The whole family got to know me very well.

Grandpa said, "Do not leave your host's house throwing mud in his well." It means that when you meet new people or are invited by people you don't know well, don't look for the bad side of them, but look for the good. Bob and Connie were so loving and fun to be with.

When the four-year-old was so curious about my dirty face, I never got offended. Grandpa taught us that "what has been blown away cannot be found again." You see, when the four-year-old girl was asking the question about my dirty face, I could have been angry, and I would have not been with the family at all.

Note this from Grandpa: "Even an ant may harm an elephant." We have to watch our words when we speak.

Finally, Bob and Connie asked me if I could be a babysitter to watch the four well-behaved kids. I did, and they became friends, and I taught them African stories.

The Corey family made me feel welcome when I was going to the academy. They introduced me to many people in Canton. Today when I go to Canton for a visit, Connie tells people that I am coming. When I get to Canton, people go out telling others that the mayor of Canton is in town, and they know it's me.

Also, during the summer when I was babysitting the Corey children, I used to sit outside in downtown Canton with the Norwegians. We all talked about the memories of the Old Country by telling stories. They used to turn to me and say, "Nick, tell us stories from Kenya." I did, and at the end they would say, "Your last name sounds Norwegian."

My response to them always was, "I am the only black Norwegian in the world."

My writing about these stories is to say that we cannot succeed alone, and nobody ever has, and nobody ever will. So two or four are better than one, and a threefold cord is not easily broken.

The Sighting of a Dream

I will never forget August 2, 1962, at ten in the morning, the first time I was coaching Benjamin to sell sewing machines door-to-door. As we walked in the streets of Nairobi City, I turned to Benjamin with a big smile and asked him, "Do you know any schools in the United States?" Very quietly, he pulled from his pocket a little black book and wrote down Augustana Academy.

I had the desire to come to school in the United States, and I wanted it so badly that I could not even spend a day without imagining coming to school in the United States. When we really have a dream or desire, we think of it day and night, and no one can tell us that we cannot achieve it. If they tell you that you cannot achieve it, you become deaf, and you move on working to achieve your dream.

When people discouraged me, it was a reminder that they had no purpose or dreams to achieve themselves, and I paid even more attention to my dream to come to school at the Augustana Academy.

I had no alternative but to make it to school at the academy to achieve my dream in education and to eventually operate my own business. We have to respond to the truth of our desire and discover our rightful position in life instead of just wishing.

Let's search our hearts for what our dreams are. We need to find our purpose, mission, or passion in life and then apply inspired actions to make our dreams come true.

Many people give up on their dreams and accept mediocrity. Don't ever let anybody say you cannot do something, not even me. Many people give up on their dreams because people doubt them. What I found to keep your dream alive is to turn the criticism and negative responses around and use those thoughts as fuel for the fire.

Dream big. The ultimate dream should be unreasonable and senseless. If it is not, you are not really dreaming big enough. When we have a dream that is big enough, it will be totally mind blowing. It will be one that challenges you and scares you at the same time. It will be a dream that is so big you will get excited and question your own sanity at the same time.

To accomplish great things, we must not only dream and act, but also believe. Our beliefs constitute such a big part of who we are; we are what we believe.

I remember walking miles and miles to get the shots I needed to enter the United States because I had no money to ride a bus. Still my dream was to come to school. I thought about and imagined coming to school at the academy every day. I visualized it every day. I prayed to God three or four times a day to open a door for me and show me the proper path I should take so that I could attend school.

My spiritual faith guided me to believe and take actions. To believe what you do not know is faith. Faith is the giving of complete trust to someone or something else in the belief that it will produce relief or benefit.

> Thoughts about faith:
> Faith is trust in the higher power to get right the conditions of our lives.
> Faith provides us access to a power that ordinary life cannot possibly provide.
> Faith brings peace and joy as we are sure that the Divine will work on our behalf.
> Faith is spiritual knowledge reflected in the mind.
> Faith is not just trust in the Highest Power to set right the conditions of our lives, but the joy in opening to and surrendering to the will of the infinite divine.
>
> —Roy Posner

When hope and faith become empty, our dreams are gone.

Don't quit until your assignment is done. You will face challenges along the way. Think about this: If you are building a house and a nail breaks, do you stop building, or do you change the nail? Of course you have to change the nail. When challenges face you in building a business, you don't stop; you find a new approach and continue building your business or anything else you want.

Sometimes you will face pain, but keep on applying actions and persistence. Press on even when you feel like quitting. Do you want to know who you are? Act! Action will delineate and define you.

Note that an intelligent enemy is better than a person who quits after a challenge. When I was struggling to come to school in the United States, I faced a lot of challenges. I wanted to design my own life in education and work for myself. Jim Rohn said, "If you don't design your own life plan, chances are you'll fall into someone else's plan."

I have found out that nothing worthwhile comes easily; you have to work for it. Any dream worth dreaming is worth the effort to make it happen.

Sometimes people ask me, where did you find the courage to follow your dreams? I found the courage because the alternative was scary. Being stuck in a dead-end job, working for a wage with two weeks a year of holidays, having my career float on the whims and fancy of a boss or management team—by comparison, being an entrepreneur seemed the least scary of my options.

The courage to follow your dreams really has to come from within yourself. I gained the courage to follow my dreams growing up, having lots of people telling me that my dreams were pointless. Eventually I realized that it was better to trust in myself and not to listen to all the negativity out there.

I have found that our quality of life will be determined by our ability to fully express the drive we feel boiling inside. Deep down, whatever you know you can be, you must be. You have the power of the dream and the courage to achieve anything you want badly enough to work for.

Courage for five years of struggle and action made my dream come true. A wise Eddie Rickenbacker once said, "Courage is doing what you are afraid to do. There can be no courage unless you are scared."

Alan Cohen said it best:

> It takes a lot of courage to release the familiar and seemingly secure, to embrace the new. But there is no real security in what is no longer meaningful. There is more security in the adventurous and exciting, for in movement there is life, and in change there is power.

Finally, our associations are some of the most powerful factors in determining who we become and what we accomplish. As an example, if we hang out with pessimistic people who are critical of our creative forward thinking, their negative comments will likely impact how we view our abilities and our image. Jim Polm said, "You will become the combined average of the five people you hang around the most. You will have their combined attitude, health, and income."

We must find mentors whom we trust and love. Having someone who can relate to the path you are on and guide you on the way means more than anything in the world. The extra layer of motivation and encouragement will further incline you to continue on this unusual journey of pursuing your dreams. The person will keep you on track and hold you accountable for the goals you set. Remember that experience is the best teacher. It's through experience that you are able to forge wonderful relationships with people who can greatly help you along the way. Life without mentorship is useless, as you will have no one whom you can look up to for guidance and advice. Mentorship is a huge factor in terms of reaching and achieving great success.

It is also important that you help others learn and grow. You can do this through a mentoring partnership. Mentoring is sharing your knowledge and experience and encouraging and motivating others.

Erma Bombeck said it simply in a profound quote:

> There are people who put their dreams in a little box and say, "Yes, I've got dreams, of course I've got dreams." Then they put the box away and bring it out once in a while to look in it, and yep, they're still there. These are great dreams, but they never even get out of the box. It takes an uncommon amount of guts to put your dreams on the line, to hold them up and say, "How good or how bad am I?" That's where courage comes in.

Our greatest responsibility in life is to encourage everyone in the same manner as my parents and grandparents encouraged my siblings and me over the course of our lives.

An old Cherokee told his grandson, "My son, there is a battle between two wolves inside us all. One is evil. It is anger, jealousy, greed, resentment, inferiority, lies, and ego. The other is good. It is hope, joy, peace, love, humility, kindness, empathy, and truth."

The boy thought about it and asked, "Grandfather, which wolf wins?"

The old man quietly replied, "The one you feed."

Are you feeding your mind and heart with positive things? Are you building relationships, courage, action, faith, and dreams?

Grandpa Tumbo said, "When a needle falls into a deep well, many people will look into the well, but few will be ready to go down after it."

If you have a dream, go into the well to get the needle by your actions and nothing less.

TRUE DIRECTIONS
An affiliate of Tarcher Books

OUR MISSION

Tarcher's mission has always been to publish books
that contain great ideas. Why? Because:

GREAT LIVES BEGIN WITH GREAT IDEAS

At Tarcher, we recognize that many talented authors, speakers,
educators, and thought-leaders share this mission and deserve to be
published – many more than Tarcher can reasonably publish ourselves.
True Directions is ideal for authors and books that increase awareness,
raise consciousness, and inspire others to live their ideals and passions.

Like Tarcher, True Directions books are designed to do three things:
inspire, inform, and motivate.

Thus, True Directions is an ideal way for these important voices
to bring their messages of hope, healing, and help to the world.

Every book published by True Directions– whether it is non-
fiction, memoir, novel, poetry or children's book – continues
Tarcher's mission to publish works that bring positive
change in the world. We invite you to join our mission.

For more information, see the True Directions website:
www.iUniverse.com/TrueDirections/SignUp

Be a part of Tarcher's community to bring positive
change in this world! See exclusive author videos, discover
new and exciting books, learn about upcoming events,
connect with author blogs and websites, and more!
www.tarcherbooks.com

TRUE DIRECTIONS
AN AFFILIATE OF TARCHER BOOKS

Printed in the United States
By Bookmasters